GRAZIERS AND GRASSLANDS
Portrait of a Rural Meath Community 1854–1914

Maynooth Studies in Local History

GENERAL EDITOR Raymond Gillespie

This is one of six new pamphlets published in 1998 in the Maynooth Studies in Local History series. Like their fourteen predecessors these volumes illustrate, through case studies of particular areas and themes, how life in Ireland in the past evolved in a variety of settings, both urban and rural. As such they join a rapidly growing literature dealing with the local dimension of Ireland's past. That 'localness' is not primarily territorial, although all are firmly rooted in a sense of place, but derives from an awareness of the regional diversity of Irish society in the past.

Local history is not about administrative frameworks or geographical entities but rather about the people who created the social worlds which made particular places distinctive. These pamphlets are therefore primarily about people who lived in particular places over time. The range of people explored is wide; from the poor of pre-famine Drogheda and Ferbane through the nouveau riche world of the Meath grazier to the aristocratic lifestyle of an eighteenth-century Tipperary landlord. What all these people have in common is that they shaped their particular places in response to stimuli both from within their communities and from the wider world.

Like their predecessors these pamphlets allow us a brief glimpse into the diverse, interacting worlds which are the basis of the Irish historical experience. In their own right they are each significant contributions to our understanding of that experience in all its richness and complexity. They present local history as the vibrant and challenging discipline that it is.

Maynooth Studies in Local History: Number 16

Graziers and Grasslands

Portrait of a Rural Meath Community 1854–1914

Jim Gilligan

IRISH ACADEMIC PRESS

First published in 1998 by
IRISH ACADEMIC PRESS
44, Northumberland Road, Dublin 4, Ireland
and in North America by
IRISH ACADEMIC PRESS
c/o ISBS, 5804 NE Hassalo Street, Portland, OR 97213
website: http://www.iap.ie

© Jim Gilligan 1998

British Library Cataloguing in Publication Data

Gilligan, Jim
   Graziers and grasslands: portrait of a rural Meath community, 1854–1914. – (Maynooth studies in local history)
   1. Farmers – Ireland – Dunshaughlin – History – 19th
   century 2. Farmers – Ireland – Dunshaughlin – History
   – 20th century
   I. Title
   630. 9'41822'09034

   ISBN 0–7165–2699–9

Typeset in 10 pt on 12 pt Bembo by
Carrigboy Typesetting Services, County Cork
Printed by ColourBooks Ltd., Dublin

Contents

FIGURES

NOTE ON UNITS OF MEASUREMENT

Unless otherwise stated an acre refers to a statute acre. Irish acres may be converted to statute acres by multiplying by a factor of 1.62.

The pre-decimal units of currency were pounds (£), shillings (s.) and pence (d.), written thus, £. s. d. For the reader wishing to convert to decimal currency a shilling, which contained twelve old pennies, is equivalent to 5 decimal pence and 20 shillings is equivalent to a pound.

Preface

Thanks are due to many people and institutions for their help in facilitating research; The National Archives; The National Library of Ireland; The Registry of Deeds; The Valuation Office; The Library, National University of Ireland, Maynooth; Meath County Library, Navan; and Louth County Library, Stockwell Street, Drogheda. I also record my gratitude to the following for access to records in their possession: Fr. John Kerrane, P.P. Dunshaughlin; the principals of Culmullen and Dunshaughlin National Schools, Mrs. Kathleen Noone and Mr. Charles Gallagher respectively; Mr. Brendan Murray and Mr. Michael Delany, Dunshaughlin. Thanks also to Louis McEntaggart for his invaluable advice on material in the Registry of Deeds. I am particularly grateful to Mickey Kenny of Dunshaughlin for sharing his invaluable information on, and insights into the area.

I am indebted to Dr. Carla King for her expert advice, suggestions and support. I also wish to record my appreciation to Dr. Mary Ann Lyons and Dr. Raymond Gillespie of the Department of Modern History in Maynooth for their guidance and advice. Finally, I thank my colleagues on the 1995–7 M.A. course in local history for the interchange of ideas and opinions and practical advice.

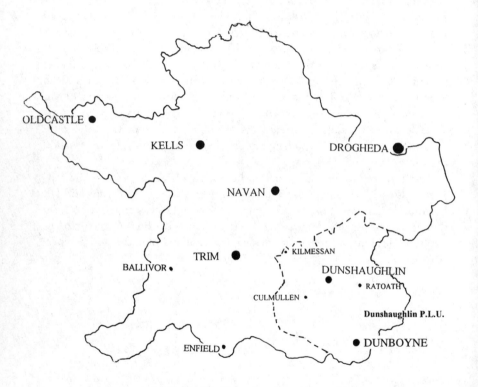

1. County Meath showing places mentioned in the text.

Introduction

Writing to the *Drogheda Independent* at the beginning of this century, Bernard Carolan, a local shopkeeper and political activist, described Dunshaughlin as 'rapidly reverting to a howling wilderness,' due, he maintained, to the profusion of immense grazing ranches which required little or no farm labour.[1] William Bulfin in his popular *Rambles in Eirinn* published in 1907, described the area as 'a lovely wilderness of grass – a verdant fertile desert from which man had banished himself and into which he had sent the beasts to take his place.'[2] Such views may have been colourfully expressed but they reflected the reality of a massive decline in population. By 1911, 897 people lived in a rural area where in 1851 a total of 2,025 resided. The pre-Famine figure had been higher still at 2,697. (See Table 1).

Whereas the slump in population from 1841 to 1851 may be accounted for by the impact of the Great Famine, the relentless continuation of the decline during the post-Famine era is linked to ongoing economic and social change in the area. In the period from the aftermath of the Famine to the onset of the first world war the farming community in the Dunshaughlin area of south east Meath experienced significant change in the distribution and ownership of farmland and the type of farming practised. Tillage acreages diminished as farmers turned in increasing numbers to grazing for beef production and as the grazier prospered the demand for labour declined. This changeover from a tillage to a grassland economy had major implications for population and this book attempts to explore and analyse the impact of those changes on the farming community of the area.

The period 1854–1914 was characterised by great dissension and conflict on the issue of land as well as by numerous attempts to reform and amend the prevailing system. It was an era marked by legislation to deal with incumbered estates, with the relationship between landlord and tenant and with labourers' accommodation. Some elements of legislation impinged directly on the inhabitants and led to change; others failed to disrupt long established patterns of living and farming. This survey will explore the extent of continuity and change, focusing on three groups, the large graziers, the medium sized farmers with less than 100 acres and the agricultural labourers.

Much has been written on the land question in the nineteenth century, but usually on a national basis or on areas which suffered upheaval and conflict, with the emphasis on the landlords and small tenants. Less has been published about the experience of extensive or substantial farmers, found especially in eastern areas, and the communities they inhabited. W. E. Vaughan has written an article on the career of a Dunshaughlin grazier in 'Farmer, grazier and gentleman: Edward Delany of Woodtown, 1851–99'[3] and Delany looms large in this work. David Seth Jones in *Graziers, land reform and political conflict in Ireland* has given an illuminating account of this type of farming on a national basis.[4] It is hoped that the present work will add further insights to a neglected area of Irish history.

The parish of Dunshaughlin (Figure 2) is a complex administrative entity which compounds the historian's task. The Roman Catholic parish of Dunshaughlin consists of three civil parishes, Dunshaughlin, Culmullen and Knockmark, it overlaps three baronies, Upper and Lower Deece and Ratoath and it is spread over three electoral divisions, Dunshaughlin, Culmullen and Killeen. Thus, the collection of statistics and official data can involve research over a wide area. Nevertheless, the main focus of this study is the Catholic parish and particularly the rural portion of it, as it is a long standing entity with which people associate and which provided focal points such as church, schools and parish hall. However it will be necessary at times to broaden the scope and look beyond those boundaries to a wider canvas involving neighbouring townlands, and, for statistical purposes, the poor law union.

The nineteenth-century town of Dunshaughlin was a single long street with little or no development off it and it retained its linear character well into the present century. Situated seventeen miles north west of Dublin city centre with the market town of Navan a further ten miles away it was dominated by its much larger neighbours and never developed as a commercial or business centre during the century. A mid century account of the town records it as 'so greatly decayed as to become a mere village.'[5]

The bulk of the parish of Dunshaughlin extended to the west of the town encompassing 14,140 acres of top quality agricultural land in forty-four townlands. These ranged in size from Culmullen's 1,266 acres and Woodtown's 947 to Grangend with less than ten and Merrywell with sixteen. The soil was generally rich and fertile, the area was close to Dublin with its markets and consequently to overseas outlets and also in close proximity were the market towns of Navan and Trim and the port of Drogheda.

The Primary Valuation of Ireland, better known as Griffith's Valuation, gives us an indication of the value ascribed to land all over Ireland. Griffith valued land 'according to the nature and depth of the soil, and the quality of the subsoil, all the local circumstances being taken into consideration' and at the 'rate it would reasonably let for by lease to a solvent tenant, on a lease of 21 years'.[6]

Griffith's valuation of Dunshaughlin was published in 1854 and the average value for each townland is summarized in Figure 3. Only in one townland, Redbog, did the valuation fall below 10 shillings per acre while great swathes of land were assessed at over £1 per acre. The townlands of Baronstown,

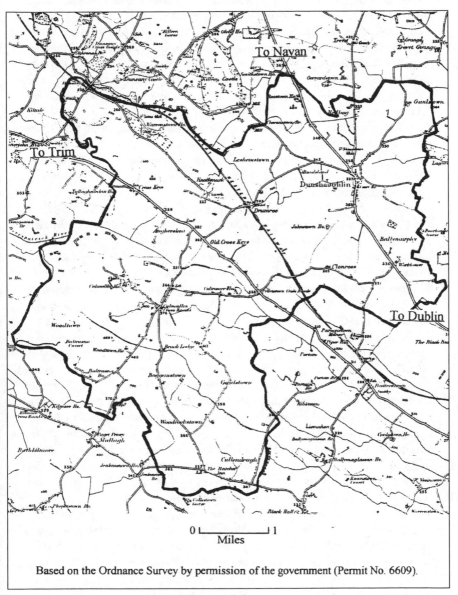

Based on the Ordnance Survey by permission of the government (Permit No. 6609).

2. Dunshaughlin Roman Catholic parish

Bedfanstown, Bonestown, Cooksland, Culmullen, Derrockstown, Grangend, Hayestown, Knockmark, Leshamstown, Merrywell, Mooretown, Roestown and both Warrenstowns were all so valued. Such valuable land amounted in all to 5,414 acres or over 38 per cent of the total acreage.

The average valuation per acre for the parish was 18s. 3d. Only eight town-lands dropped below 15s. – Ballinlough, Ballymurphy, Culcommon, Drumree, Glane Little, Pelletstown, Redbog and Woodcockstown, a total of 1,657 acres representing 12 per cent of the parish. Indeed many of these townlands were close to the 15 shillings value with Redbog the only one whose rating reflected poor fertility.

These figures were high when compared with other areas. David Seth Jones calculated average values per acre of 8s., 7s. and 1s. for the Poor Law unions of Athlone, Tulla (County Clare), and Belmullet respectively.[7] Nolan's study of a County Kilkenny barony records 28 per cent of it at 12s. or over whereas in Dunshaughlin parish the corresponding figure was 98 per cent.[8] A return of valuation completed by 1852 gives an average valuation per acre of 18s. 5d. for Meath with most counties well below this. Neighbouring counties Westmeath and Kildare were rated at 14s. and 13s. 10d. respectively. Only Louth with 19s. 2d. exceeded Meath while all counties west of the Shannon fell below 10s.[9] By such criteria Dunshaughlin was highly valued as were adjacent parishes. Killeen averaged 19s. 7d., Rathbeggan 18s., Rathregan 19s. 2d. and Trevet an unusually high £1. 2s. 5d.[10] so the parish lay in the centre of one of the most fertile agricultural areas in the country.

Despite this apparent prosperity the Famine had a significant impact on the area. While eastern counties like Meath did not experience the levels of starvation, death and depopulation suffered along the western seaboard, never-theless Meath's population fell by 23 per cent between 1841 and 1851. This was average for the country as a whole but significantly above the Leinster average of 15 per cent. The overall figures tend of course to disguise regional variation, and population decline within Meath varied with location. The northern baronies such as Kells Lower, Morgallion and Slane Lower experienced drops of 39 per cent, 37 per cent and 34 per cent respectively whereas those in the south such as Dunboyne, Navan Upper and Ratoath were less severely hit with declines of 7 per cent, 13 per cent and 14 per cent.[11]

The 1841 census recorded a population for Dunshaughlin parish of 3,221 which dropped to 2,447 ten years later, a decline of 24 per cent, just above county average and well above average for the barony of Ratoath. Just as global county figures may disguise variations and patterns within the county so also with the parish and accordingly it is instructive to look at smaller units within it. If one examines the figures for the three civil parishes and the town of Dunshaughlin separately one important trend is apparent. (Table 1).

In 1841 and throughout the nineteenth century the bulk of the population resided in the rural areas. The town had a population of 524 in 1841,

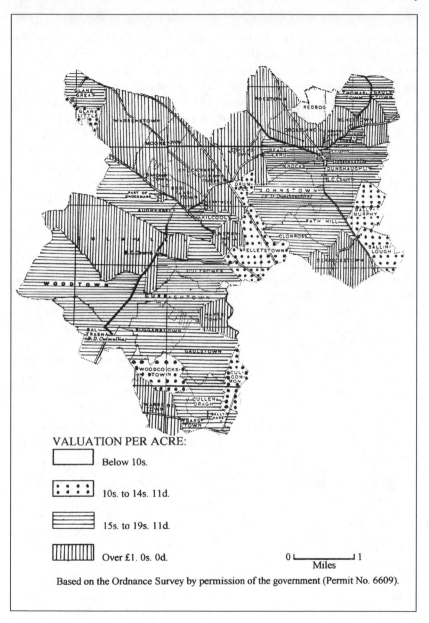

VALUATION PER ACRE:

Below 10s.

10s. to 14s. 11d.

15s. to 19s. 11d.

Over £1. 0s. 0d.

0 |_____| 1
Miles

Based on the Ordnance Survey by permission of the government (Permit No. 6609).

3. Valuation of land by townland, Griffith's Valuation 1854

Dunshaughlin civil parish had double this with 1,057, Culmullen was close to double at 1,010 and even the smallest civil parish, Knockmark, recorded a figure of 630. When the Famine struck it affected the rural area much more severely than the town. The latter fell to 422 in 1851 a decline of 19.5 per cent whereas the areas outside the town declined overall by 25 per cent. Dunshaughlin civil parish, excluding the town, dropped 29.5 per cent and Culmullen and Knockmark fell by 25.4 per cent and 16.4 per cent respectively. This was a pattern which was to repeat itself throughout the century and Knockmark which declined less steeply than the other rural areas initially would match their decline later. By 1901 the population of the four constituent parts of the parish had achieved a rough equality in numbers as the pattern of rural depopulation evident in 1851 intensified for the remainder of the century. The reasons for this will be analysed in later chapters. At the townland level variations can be observed also. (See Appendix 2 for full details). Few townlands increased in population over the Famine decade, those few which did had a low initial base and the increases were usually due to extra families moving in. Clonross for example rose from sixteen to thirty-seven, accounted for by a doubling of the number of houses from two to four. The townlands most affected by the decline and the percentage drops experienced were, Merrywell 66.7 per cent, Cooksland 61.7 per cent, Dunshaughlin 48.5 per cent and Roestown 25 per cent, all in Dunshaughlin civil parish. In Culmullen parish Culmullen fell 45.1 per cent, Woodcockstown 44.9 per cent, Bogganstown 44.1 per cent and Woodtown 38 per cent while in Knockmark parish the figures were Drumree 63 per cent, Mooretown 56 per cent and Augherskea 26.6 per cent.

Table 1. Population of Civil Parishes and Town, 1841–1911

	Dunsh'lin Town	Dunsh'lin Civil Parish	Culmullen	Knockmark
1841	524	1,057	1,010	630
1851	422	745	753	527
1861	403	610	568	469
1871	362	465	512	320
1881	354	382	453	286
1891	291	336	408	290
1901	315	333	335	272
1911	265	388	270	239

Note: The data for Dunshaughlin civil parish excludes residents of the Workhouse as they came from all over the union.
Source: Decennial census returns for the period 1841 to 1911.

It is not immediately clear why these townlands were so severely hit. Figures from small samples can skew trends, but a few observations may be made. In general these townlands contained good quality, highly rated land, particularly Cooksland, Culmullen, Dunshaughlin, Merrywell, Roestown and Woodtown, all valued at over 18s. per acre. Only Drumree and Woodcockstown had relatively low valuations. It may be that many of the inhabitants of the highly valued townlands in the pre-Famine era were, in the main, labourers dependent for work on the land and as conditions disimproved during the Famine the landlords may have been unable or unwilling to provide work as previously. Lacking employment such labourers would have little choice but to depart. Secondly, the trend towards grazing and cattle farming and away from tillage which was gathering pace by mid-century and which was beginning to monopolize the rich grasslands of Meath would have meant less employment on farms. Grazing was to become the dominant mode of farming as the century progressed and it required a low labour input. This aspect is treated more fully in later chapters.

The situation in the poorest townland was in marked contrast. Redbog, one mile north-east of Dunshaughlin consisting of 209 acres of mainly wet, unproductive and as its name implies, boggy land, housed a population of 145 in 1841, living in twenty-six houses. The next decade brought little change. In 1851, 132 people still eked out a living here but more significantly the number of dwellings had reached thirty-two. The poor land was not an attractive proposition for graziers and so there was very little clearance in Redbog, it is likely instead that subdivision continued, probably for existing family members. This parish in the main, was an area of highly valued agricultural land which experienced a big decrease in population after the Famine. It was a decrease which, in general, afflicted the rural parts, especially the richer townlands while poorer ones like Redbog and the town itself were not as acutely affected.

In addition to assessing land values Griffith's Valuation also gives a snapshot of the pattern of landholding in the area at mid-century. An analysis of Griffith's returns reveals that no one landlord dominated the parish and accordingly no one emerged to shape and dictate developments. In addition, the majority of the large landowners resided outside the parish and apart from leasing the land for various terms few of them had a regular, ongoing involvement in the area. Thus, though a large percentage of the land was owned by a few powerful landlords they exerted very little direct influence or control over the parish.[12]

Hans Hamilton Woods (1814–1879) was the dominant landholder near the town. The Woods family held land in Dunshaughlin throughout the eighteenth century but Woods spent most of his time in Balbriggan, the ancestral home and the Dunshaughlin lands were leased. In all, Woods held over 1,300 acres mainly in Johnstown, Leshemstown and Roestown but held less than an acre in the town.[13] Thomas E. Taylor, a brother-in-law of Woods and a cousin of the marquess of Headfort in Kells, had over 600 acres, owning all of Bonestown,

Gaulstown and Thomastown but he lived in Ardgillan Castle at Balbriggan and held over 7,000 acres in total in Meath. He represented County Dublin as M.P. from 1841 to 1883.[14] Henry White, who became the first Baron Annaly in 1863, had holdings in excess of 1,000 acres, all in Culmullen and Knockmark parishes and as much again in neighbouring parishes. He appears to have purchased the lands from Lord Bessborough early in the nineteenth century, and had residences in Luttrellstown, County Dublin and Rathcline, County Longford, both of which counties he represented as M.P.[15] The Supples, who had 500 acres, had a lengthy association with the town and were active in the Church of Ireland, yet by 1862 Frederick Supple resided at Mount Merrion in Dublin.[16]

Two families long associated with the area, the earls of Fingall and the Husseys also held extensive tracts of land in the parish though both resided outside it, Fingall just three miles from Dunshaughlin in Killeen Castle and the Husseys in Slane. Fingall was a member of the Plunket family who had a presence in the area from the thirteenth century while the Husseys were among the earliest Norman families to settle in Meath. Fingall held almost 10,000 acres in Meath while the Husseys held upwards of 3,000 acres. Accordingly their Dunshaughlin possessions were rarely the prime focus of their concerns.

One of the largest and most valuable holdings of land in the parish belonged to Samuel Dopping, including all of the townlands of Culmullen and Woodtown. A Samuel Dopping is recorded in the late seventeenth-century Books of Survey and Distribution as owning the land here but by 1850, just prior to the period covered in this book, the whole estate was sold in the Incumbered Estates Court.[17] The Knox and Wilson families owned large tracts of land in the parish, between them they held all of Bedfanstown, Clonross, and Cultromer and practically all of Derrockstown, amounting to about 1,000 acres but evenly spread between Mabel Tucker (nee Wilson), Jane Wilson, Arthur Knox and Rev. George Knox. They leased all the land and did not live in the parish.

The Johnsons of Warrenstown and Knockmark were a long established family. In Griffith's Valuation, Eliza M. Johnson is recorded as the holder of almost 1,000 acres and the family was the biggest landholder to reside in the parish, holding all of the townlands of Warrenstown, Kilcooley, Drumree and Baronstown. She held 673 of those acres in fee and it is probable that the Johnsons farmed those themselves.

Thus the landowners were, in the main, absentees, often with more substantial interests elsewhere, and families which had been resident in the early nineteenth century like the Woods and Supples moved out. Others were to sell and depart also as the century progressed, with over 35 per cent of the land in the parish for sale in the Incumbered Estates Court. Before looking at the changes in ownership which occurred as a result of those sales it is necessary to place them in their social and economic context, an issue explored in the next chapter.

Land and Agriculture after the Famine

Griffith's Valuation of 1854, and the revised or cancelled land books which record the change in farm size and ownership thereafter, allow one to compare and contrast the distribution of land in the 1850s and 1910s. Thus it is possible to assess the extent of change and continuity in the parish over sixty years. In 1854 in the rural parts of the parish 24.4 per cent of all holdings consisted of a house with no land attached, while over half, 56.4 per cent in all, were less than five acres. At the other end of the scale only 9 per cent of the farms were in excess of 100 acres. There were forty-five such holdings but between them they accounted for 59 per cent of the land in the parish, much of it leased from the large landowners mentioned in the first chapter and some of it in the ownership of the occupiers.

A number of people held more than one farm over 100 acres in size, so the forty-five farms were occupied by thirty-seven individuals. (See Appendix 3). These farms underwent limited changes in occupancy and ownership over the next half century but as Table 2 shows the number of such farms remained relatively stable. In 1911 there were thirty-nine farms in this category and the majority had undergone little or no change in size in the sixty years. Indeed the majority of the farms remained in the same family in addition to retaining their original extent.

This element of stability and continuity was in stark contrast to the position of the smallholders. Whereas 116 were recorded as living in a house without land in the rural areas in 1854, by 1911 there were only thirty-three, a huge drop of 72 per cent. The number of holdings of less than an acre – not all with a house – showed a smaller drop from fifty-one to forty-one while those on one to five acres increased slightly from 101 to 109. The latter two categories were boosted by the fact that thirty-three labourers' cottages were erected by Dunshaughlin Rural District Council up to 1911. Overall, residents in a house without land represented 24 per cent of all holdings in 1854 but by 1911 they accounted for a mere 8.5 per cent.

Those figures imply that the population decline referred to in the first chapter, which affected the rural parts much more severely than the town, was due in the main to the disappearance of the rural landless labourer. An examination of Griffith's Valuation for the parish shows that many of the occupants of such holdings were subletting from the large occupiers and obviously depended primarily on farm work on the lessor's farm due to the

Table 2. Numbers and size of rural holdings, 1854 and 1911

| | 1854 | | 1911 | |
	Total	Percentage	Total	Percentage
House only	116	24.4	33	8.5
Below 1 acre	51	10.7	41	10.6
1 to 5 acres	101	21.3	109	28.1
5 to 15 acres	67	14.1	65	16.8
15 to 30 acres	30	6.3	31	7.9
30 to 50 acres	29	6.1	32	8.2
50 to 100 acres	36	7.6	38	9.8
Over 100 acres	45	9.5	39	10.1
Total	**475**	**100**	**388**	**100**

Source: Calculations based on *General valuation of rateable property in Ireland, Union of Dunshaughlin, valuation of the several tenements,* (Dublin, 1854), pp 7–13, 42, 44–52 for 1854 and Valuation Office, Revised valuation books, Poor law union (rural district) of Dunshaughlin, no. 4, Dunshaughlin ED, no. 1, Culmullen ED, and no. 1, Killeen ED, up to 1911.

lack of local industrial and commercial activity. However, the pattern of farming and consequently the type of work available on farms underwent substantial change in the period under review as the large scale farmers switched to grazing and fattening beef cattle. This had implications for the labourer as grazing was much less labour intensive than tillage.

Grazing and the cattle economy became a central feature of post-Famine agriculture and Meath and neighbouring eastern counties were in the vanguard of the changeover to grass. There is evidence that such change even predated the Famine. A witness stated in evidence to an 1833 parliamentary committee that 'every year a great quantity of land [in Meath and Kildare] is put into grass'[1] while for an 1837 commission the Rev. G.L. Irvine, Church of Ireland clergyman for Dunshaughlin, categorized the local landlords as 'farmers and graziers'.[2]

From 1847 agricultural statistics were collected by the Royal Irish Constabulary and published as parliamentary papers. Those provide detailed evidence of the change away from tillage farming and a huge expansion in grassland. Meath was consistently to the fore as the county with the greatest proportion of its area under grassland and the district round Dunshaughlin reflected this. Unfortunately the format used in reporting the statistics varied and the only unit which was consistently used in the 1847–1911 period was the Poor Law Union. Accordingly it is the main unit chosen here for comparative purposes but I have also used statistics from the barony when appropriate.

The parish of Dunshaughlin is in the centre of Dunshaughlin poor law union and comprises 13 per cent of the union's area. Although one cannot assume that figures at union level reflect accurately the reality within any section of the union, nevertheless it can be asserted that such figures are very valuable in indicating the overall trends and patterns of farming within the parish. Furthermore, the statistics reveal a pattern so consistent and strong it is unlikely a substantial section of the union like Dunshaughlin deviated from it, while evidence from barony, parish and individual farm level confirm the trends at union level.

Table 3 shows the wheat, oats, potatoes, total tillage and grassland acreages for 1851–1911 at five year intervals. Figures for 1851 and each subsequent tenth year were included to maintain the decennial pattern of the census of population reports for comparative purposes. Tillage shows a dramatic decline.[3] In the forty years from 1851 to 1891 it dropped from over 24,000 acres to just over 4,000, a massive decrease of 82.5 per cent. Wheat growing practically disappeared from the union, the 1891 figure was only 3 per cent of the 1851 return. Oats fared a little better, retaining 15 per cent of the 1851 figure by 1891. Potato growing which was minimal in Black '47 but improved in the post Famine 1850s, had halved again by the turn of the century.

There was a corresponding increase in the acreage devoted to grassland, expanding from 63,762 acres or 58 per cent of the Union in 1851 to a high of

Table 3. Tillage and Grassland Acreages, Dunshaughlin P.L.U. 1851–1911

	wheat	Oats	Potatoes	Total tillage	Grassland
1851	4947	14791	1439	24112	63762
1856	4435	10708	2168	19248	69786
1861	1457	9399	1825	14404	73512
1866	1526	7389	1662	11886	73760
1871	1320	5600	1750	9980	75902
1876	382	3868	1206	6490	80140
1881	443	3328	1162	5847	79381
1886	260	2717	1093	4890	81957
1891	153	2175	1083	4205	84181
1896	67	1851	867	3427	85149
1901	90	1434	757	2970	87199
1906	111	1363	647	2844	85966
1911	128	1489	695	3121	86111

Figures for 1851 from *Census of Ireland 1851, pt. ii, returns of agricultural produce in 1851,* for 1856 from *Returns of agricultural produce in Ireland in the year 1856* and 1861 onwards from *Agricultural statistics of Ireland* compiled annually. Grassland acreages for 1856–1876 are the author's estimates based on the returns.

87,199 or 81.6 per cent of the land in 1901.[4] As the proportion of land under tillage plummeted the area devoted to grassland increased from an already substantial base. The drop in the acreage devoted to all crops from 1851 to 1911 was 20,991 while the increase in grassland at 22,349 acres was very close to this, indicating that practically all the land which ceased to produce tillage was converted to grassland. (Table 3).

The transfer of land from tillage to grass was a national phenomenon in the second half of the nineteenth century. In Ireland as a whole the tillage acreage dropped from 4,612,543 in 1851 to 2,334,776 in 1911, a drop of 48 per cent.[5] Meath, and in particular the Dunshaughlin Union were the foremost in Ireland in this change, with tillage acreage falling 78 per cent and 87 per cent respectively.[6] Table 4 shows the five unions with the highest proportion of land under grass from 1871 to 1911 at ten year intervals. Dunshaughlin always held first place in the country. In general it exceeded its nearest rivals by up to 15 per cent, chief among which were the other Meath unions of Kells, Navan and Trim. In 1901, for example, a figure of 81.6 per cent grassland was recorded, the next highest was Navan with 72.4 per cent and no other union exceeded 70 per cent.

The changeover to pasture was paralleled by a burgeoning of the cattle population which is shown graphically in Figure 2. Meath was the centre of the grazing district of Ireland whose function was to fatten store cattle (generally two years and older) for the Dublin, Drogheda and English markets. The numbers of such cattle in the Dunshaughlin union increased from 19,009 in 1851 to 35,687 in 1911 with the high point being the 1901 figure of 38,184, double the initial total. The greatest spurt occurred in the 1851–61 period, a jump of 35.7 per cent which took place at a time of rising prices, which will be referred to later. Looking at a smaller area like the barony of Ratoath, of which the civil parish of Dunshaughlin made up 15 per cent a similar pattern is discernible. In the barony the rate of growth was 39.7 per cent between 1851 and 1861.[7]

Table 4. Unions with greatest Proportion of Area under grass, 1881–1911

	1881		*1891*		*1901*		*1911*
Dunsh'lin	73.3	Dunsh'lin	77.8	Dunsh'lin	81.6	Dunsh'lin	80.6
Enistymon	66.6	Navan	71.4	Navan	72.4	Navan	71.4
B'Vaughan	66.0	Celbridge	68.1	Celbridge	69.7	Kells	70.4
Trim	67.3	B'vaughan	67.6	Kells	69.4	Callan	69.9
Kells	64.6	Trim	67.3	Rathkeale	69.1	Croom	68.8

Source: *Agricultural statistics of Ireland for the year 1881*, p. 21 [C 3332], H.C. 1882, lxxiv, 113, *Agricultural statistics of Ireland for the year 1891*, p. 39 [C 6777], H.C. 1892, lxxxviii, 323, *Agricultural statistics of Ireland . . . 1901*, pp 29–31 and *Agricultural statistics of Ireland . . . 1911*, pp 31–33.

4. Trend of Cattle numbers, two years and above,
Dunshaughlin P.L.U., 1851–1911

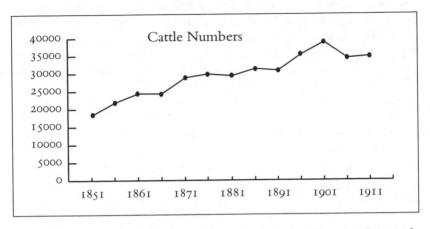

Source: Census of Ireland 1851, pt. ii: returns of agricultural produce, 1851, Returns of agricultural produce in Ireland, 1856 and Agricultural statistics of Ireland 1861 to 1911 at five year intervals. Milch cows were not recorded as a separate category until 1854. Consequently the base figure for 1851, 19,009 which includes milch cows, understates the number of two year old beef cattle so the percentage increases in the text underestimate the actual increases by a few points.

The increase in cattle numbers was accommodated by the availability of extra grassland, due to the switch from tillage, and to a lesser extent by an improved stocking rate. Calculation of stocking rates for the union suggests that the rates showed very little increase until the end of the century. For the years 1856–91 the rates were roughly forty livestock units per 100 acres while in the 1900s it had improved to over fifty units per 100 acres. (See Appendix 4).

There is little doubt that the move towards grazing in the local union and barony was replicated at parish level. Although, as explained previously, official figures for the parish do not exist, local evidence points to the predominance of grazing. The prospectuses issued to publicize the sale of estates under the Incumbered Estates Acts usually refer to the quality and use of the land. While the earliest sales in the parish in the 1850s mention the suitability of the soil for tillage, the emphasis is on grazing later in the century. An 1850 sale of Culmullen and Woodtown describes it as 'rich, arable, meadow and pasture land',[8] Derrockstown in 1861 contains 'some of the best arable, meadow and pasture land in the County of Meath'[9] and Merrywell in 1866 is 'very superior quality for either grazing or tillage.'[10] In 1870, Woodtown and Bedfanstown are 'of prime quality and all under grass with the exception of about fourteen acres',[11] Warrenstown is 'fine grazing land'[12] while in Derrockstown 'the last letting was for grazing purposes only.'[13] Part of Culmullen came up for sale again in 1885 and it is described as 'of excellent quality, old rich pasture' and 'the greater portion of the lands were let to graziers for £1,055 for the year'.[14] Local political activists were also aware of the change. Bernard Carolan, who was involved in nationalist organizations from 1880, complained in *The Drogheda Independent* in 1900 that Dunshaughlin could support an immense population but because of the huge grazing ranches and the lack of a native legislature 'the area was reverting to a howling wilderness'.[15]

In addition to this trend towards pasture there was also a big turnover in land ownership. From 1850 onwards vast tracts of land in Dunshaughlin changed hands, mainly as a result of the Incumbered Estates Acts. Many estates in Ireland were debt ridden for various reasons, such as the inability of tenants to pay rent during the Famine, the impact of the poor law rates, neglect or misman-agement of estates and the charging of annuities on the land to provide for family members who did not inherit the estate. Legislation in the late 1840s provided for such lands to be sold by the Commissioners for Incumbered Estates, later the Landed Estates Court, at the request of an owner or creditor. A detailed prospectus, often with maps and always with descriptions of the land and rentals was produced for all sales.

Between 1851 and 1885 fourteen sales took place in Dunshaughlin. In all, a total of over 5,000 acres changed hands which represented 35 per cent of the parish. The two biggest townlands in the parish, Culmullen and Woodtown both went under the Commissioners' hammer. All of Ballynare, Bedfanstown, Culcommon, Cullendragh, Derrockstown, Little Glane, Merrywell and Warrenstown (Culmullen) were also sold, along with substantial parts of Augherskea, Curraghtown, and Pelletstown.

Conflicting views have been offered by historians on the buyers of incum-bered estates. The British government had hoped that English capitalists would invest in and improve the estates but by 1857 only 4 per cent were English, Scottish or foreign.[16] The orthodox view for many years was that buyers came from a commercial background and raised rents while more recent research supports the view that the buyers were, in the main, from the established landed and professional elites, with the sellers replaced by buyers of a similar socio-economic status. The evidence from the sales in Dunshaughlin tends to support this view but a significant number of purchasers were locals, mainly men who were already renting the land while a few also came from the com-mercial sector. Table 5 summarizes all sales over fifty acres from 1850 to 1885.

The most important sale in the parish was one of the earliest under the act, the disposal of over 2,500 acres belonging to Samuel Dopping in June 1850. There was a further 1,550 acres in neighbouring parishes and the estate was debt ridden to the tune of £126,197.[17] The lands in Culmullen, Woodtown and Curraghtown contained some of the best land in the parish and the sale attracted such interest that it was held in the Rotunda, the usual venue being

Extent	Buyer	Status	Price in £	Yrs. Rental
		Culmullen 1850		
662:1:32	James Kearney	Landowner, Meath	11,600	13 (27)
343:1:14	William Gibson	Solicitor, Dublin	6,850	16 (31)
111:0:06	Patrick Leonard	Salesmaster/Farmer	2,700	20
170:3:03	Patrick Leonard	Salesmaster/Farmer	2,700	16 (39)
196:3:08	Patrick Leonard	Salesmaster/Farmer	3,445	18
145:3:29	M.E. Corbally	Landed gentry &M.P	3,545	13
126:0:31	Francis Rochfort	Provision merchant, Dublin	3,000	21
940:2:35	William Wilson	Possibly a solicitor, Dublin	3,450	22
		Culcommon, 1851		
182:2:30	Philip Grierson	Landowner, Meath	1,600	15
		Pelletstown, 1858		
169:0:06	Patrick Leonard	Salesmaster/Farmer	4,000	30
89:0:17	Baron Cloncurry	Nobility, landowner	2,147	24
		Derrockstown, 1861		
95:1:07	T. & J. Murphy	Local farmers, leasee.	3,425	26
227:3:36	Sheridans	Not known	5,650	23
		Little Glane, 1862		
73:2:24	Mr Fottrell	In trust	1,900	31
		Merrywell, 1866		
146:0:03	Hugh Gearty	Local farmer, leasee	4,230	27
		Derrockstown, 1867		
227:2:19	Sheridans	Not known	1,725	8
		Augherskea, 1867		
295:1:27	Mr. Smith	Not known	6,775	21
223:1:29	Marcus Hughes	Merchant, Dublin	6,025	21
		Augherskea, 1868		
223:1:29	Sold privately	Not known	N/A	
		Bedfanstown, Woodtown 1870		
104:1:24	Mark Delany	Farmer, leasee & D.L.	2,577	24
112:1:24	Edward Delany	Local farmer, leasee, P.L.G	2,700	22
139:0:02	Joseph Molony	Landowner, Thurles	3,425	22
253:1:01	William Molony	Landowner, Thurles	5,385	22
		Warrenstown/Cullentra' 1872		
941:0:12	James Jameson	Esquire, Balbriggan	Private sale	

Table 5. Buyers of incumbered estates, Dunshaughlin 1850–1885

Table 5. *Buyers of incumbered estates, Dunshaughlin 1850–1885 (contd.)*				
Extent	**Buyer**	**Status**	**Price in £**	**Yrs. Rental**
228:2:29	Patrick Donegan	*Derrockstown, 1884* Manufacturer, Dublin	9,150	
662:2:39	John Kearney	*Culmullen, 1885* 'Owner' of the property	20,500	14 (25)

Note: Information compiled from L.E.C. Rentals, newspaper reports of sales, mainly *Dublin Evening Post* and *Dublin Evening Mail*, and transcripts of memorials in the Registry of Deeds. Additional details on buyers' status from *Thom's* and *Slater's Directory*. The figure under Yrs. Rental is the number of years rent which the purchase price represented. The figures in brackets in the early sales represent the number of years' rental if a charge on the estate, usually in the form of a jointure, is included.

too small. A contemporary account records the presence of 'the merchant, the capitalist, the salesmaster, factor, farmer, grazier and frieze-coated man of wealth and intelligence'. The first lot of 662 acres went for £11,600 to James Kearney.[18] The Kearneys were extensive landholders in north-east Meath and served as magistrates and deputy lieutenants of the county.[19]

A further 478 acres went to Patrick Leonard whose descendants remain large farmers in the area to the present day. The Leonards were cattle salesmasters in Dublin and Liverpool with offices at Dominick Street in the former.[20] Patrick Leonard purchased another 170 acres in an 1858 sale[21] bringing his total purchases to 650 acres at a cost of £8,845, which he appears to have paid without recourse to a loan or mortgage. He was already renting some of this land as well as 400 acres in Macetown in neighbouring Skryne parish where he had a house.[22] It is likely he bought the lands for cattle fattening which fitted in with his other role as a salesmaster. By 1897 Patrick Leonard, grandson of the original Patrick, stated that he managed for clients and worked for his own profit 3,000 acres in Meath, Kildare and Dublin.[23]

Later purchasers included Joseph and William Molony who acquired 400 acres in 1870.[24] They also had another 300 acres in a neighbouring barony and are recorded as holding 3,366 acres in County Tipperary in 1876.[25] Other purchasers at the first auction included the solicitor who had carriage of the sale, William Gibson of Dublin, Francis Rochford a provision merchant of Tighe Street in Dublin and William Wilson who acquired all of Woodtown but of whom nothing is known.[26] In 1872 James Jameson of Delvin Lodge in Balbriggan purchased all of Baron Annaly's estate in Warrenstown, Woodcockstown and Cullendragh amounting to 941 acres and almost as much again in the neighbouring parishes of Kilcloon and Moynalvey.[27] The Jamesons appear to be the whiskey magnates as in 1888 the owner is recorded as John Jameson of Bow Street.[28]

In addition to such outside buyers there were a number of local purchasers at the various sales. Those were, in the main, local well-to-do farmers, often already renting farms in the vicinity, intent on land ownership and benefiting from the contemporary boom in grazing and beef farming. The best known of those, due to the survival of some of his farm account books, was Edward Delany of Woodtown whose enterprise is treated more fully in the next chapter. He leased extensively in the parish and bought 112 acres in Woodtown in 1870. His brother, Mark Delany of Navan, bought all 104 acres in Bedfanstown which he already grazed under a forty-one year lease. Both borrowed money to pay for their acquisitions, Edward needing £1,600 and Mark £1,500 from the Commissioners of Public Works to be repaid over thirty-five years.[29]

Hugh Gearty (or Geraghty) also had a lease on 122 of the 146 acres he bought in 1866. He paid £2,230 and organized a mortgage of £2,000 to cover the balance, the principal not to be called in for at least five years. He and James, probably a brother, farmed other lands within and near the parish where they 'had for many years carried on farming and grazing pursuits'.[30] Various members of the Murphy family owned and leased land in the parish. Brothers Thomas and John availed of an 1861 sale to buy ninety-five acres in Derrockstown that Thomas already held under a lease for three lives.[31] When he died in 1887 he owned 165 acres in Derrockstown and 194 in Johnstown and leased 160 acres in Cooksland and 145 in Rathill in addition to property in the town.[32]

Philip Grierson who procured 181 acres in Culcommon and Ballynare in 1851 resided in Wood Park, Dunboyne, five miles south of Dunshaughlin. He had 150 acres there and the house and buildings were valued at an impressive £26 per annum.[33] There is also evidence that other local farmers were outbid for property. J.G. Carleton, the sitting tenant bid £1,200 for eighty-seven acres in Culmullen which eventually went to Leonard for £2,700. Laurence Dunne who held 110 acres in fee at Piper Hill just outside the parish and whose daughter married Hugh Geraghty also placed a number of bids in the 1850 sale of the Dopping property.[34] Clearly many of those local buyers and bidders were men of quite substantial means.

The evidence from the sale of the incumbered estates therefore shows that the buyers were, broadly speaking, of three types. A number such as Kearney and the Molonys already held extensive estates and belonged to the gentry while there were also representatives of the Dublin business and legal world. Despite such competition a substantial number of local farmers were able to acquire title to land in the locality and a number of those were sitting tenants. The latter were, in the main, graziers, men who bought store cattle at fairs in various counties in Connacht and Leinster to fatten on the rich pasture lands of Meath and sell in the Dublin market. Their world is outlined and analysed in the next chapter.

The Graziers' World, 1854–1904

Research into the land issue has in the past, tended to concentrate on the landed gentry who held very large tracts of land and those at the opposite end of the spectrum, the small to medium tenant farmer holding his land at will, or if he was lucky, on a short term lease. Until recently less attention has been paid to the larger farmers who held substantial farms of one hundred acres and above and were much better off than the lowly tenant. Such farmers may have been absent in many of the poorer areas of nineteenth-century Ireland but they were a conspicuous element in the landscape of County Meath, especially in the post-Famine decades.[1] Edward Delany from Woodtown in Dunshaughlin parish was one of those. As a number of his farm account books survive it is proposed to use them in this chapter, in conjunction with other material such as deeds and newspaper reports, to analyse his farming methods and lifestyle, his gradual acquisition of more land and his financial and social standing in the community. Although probably more successful than some of his contemporaries his long span as an active farmer-grazier from 1850 to 1900 provides many insights into the role of men of his class, while reference will also be made to other graziers in the community to complement or contrast evidence available in the Delany documents.

The previous chapter has sketched in the context within which Delany operated. Cattle numbers were on the increase as the area of grassland expanded and there was a precipitous drop in tillage acreage. This trend was very evident in Meath, particularly in the Dunshaughlin poor law union which consistently from 1881 to 1911 had a much higher proportion of its area given over to grassland than any other union in the country. This grassland was utilized as the final stage in the fattening of beef cattle. The initial stage of production, rearing yearling and store cattle, up to two years, was centred in north Munster and east Connaught, mainly Galway and Roscommon. The next stage, that of fattening the animals for slaughter or export was done in the grasslands of north Leinster, especially Meath, but also Westmeath and Kildare. William Bulfin, who toured Ireland in the early years of this century described the land in Meath with some hyperbole as 'probably the richest land in the world. It is certainly the richest tract of land in Europe . . . In Meath cattle are fat every summer and placed on the market weeks before cattle from other districts. There is no land in Ireland will turn off so many pounds of beef to the acre.'[2] The German agriculturalist Moritz Bonn writing in 1906 summarized this type of farming on the grasslands as 'A man buys a beast cheap, lets it graze for a certain time, and sells it off at a higher price in as short a time as possible.'[3] Edward Delany was a prime example of this type of farmer.

The capital used on such farms has been described by Jones as circulating capital, that is to say it is rarely invested in long term projects or fixed assets, but in stock, and shortly afterwards realized with a maximum possible profit and reinvested again at the beginning of another cycle.[4] The grazier had only minimal requirements for labour. Most enterprises could be looked after by a herd or two and in many cases the grazier's own family could tend to the cattle. It was a constant cause of complaint in grazing areas that there was no employment for agricultural labourers. According to the secretary of the Land and Labour Association in Dunshaughlin, the graziers' main thought is 'to cut down his labour bill and do nothing himself but view from time to time the splendid way the bullocks are working for him' and 'he is the enemy of the labourer who wants employment.'[5]

The grazier was however, usually dependent on his herd. Griffith's Valuation for the parish records forty herds' houses in 1854, in the main on the bigger farms. There were three in the biggest townland, Culmullen, on farms of 343, 190 and 187 acres and five in Woodtown on farms of 209, 198, 180, 112 and 100 acres.[6] In the 1901 census thirty-three persons recorded their occupation as herd, assistant herd or shepherd.[7] It seems that some farms which were available for rent came equipped with a herd, particularly towards the end of the century when renting grassland on short terms of eleven months became popular. A number of advertisements of pasture land for rent contain such statements as 'experienced herd will take charge of stock' and 'a competent herd will take charge of the stock.'[8] Griffith's Valuation shows that a 251 acre farm in Derrockstown leased by Delany in 1854 had a herd's house and it is possible that it came with a herd already *in situ*. Such practices are confirmed by the 1893 Commission on Labour.[9] Herds were, in general, better paid than other agricultural workers. Delany's accounts, however, provide no details of his payment to herds but it is probable that he employed at least one for both his home farm on 180 acres and Bridget Delany's nearby holding of 112 acres, which he farmed, had herds' houses on the land. In 1901 John Lamb resided on land owned by Delany and gave his occupation as herd and shepherd.[10]

Edward Delany was born in 1821 and died on 17 October 1901. The Tithe Applotment Books of 1827 record William Delany as the occupier of the farm Edward held later in the century. William also occupied another forty acres while Nicholas Delany held seventy-two acres, the latter two totalled 112a. 3r. 0p. which matches the farm Bridget Delany held in Griffith's Valuation.[11] William was Edward's father but his relationship to Bridget is unclear. The Delanys held land in or near the parish from the beginning of the nineteenth century and also had links with Kilmessan, about five miles north west of Dunshaughlin.

A headstone in Kilmessan cemetery records the death of William Delany, Woodtown on 10 October 1833. Edward however is buried in Culmullen. He married Mary Barry on 21 April 1858 when he was in his late thirties and she predeceased him on 29 May 1894, aged sixty-four years. They had six children, William in 1859, Mary Lucy in 1860, Rose Anne Bridget in 1862, Andrew 1864, Margaret 1866 and Edward 1869 who eventually inherited the Woodtown land.[12]

The farms may have been held on a lease prior to 1827 as the Delanys were in occupation from that year but none could be traced in the Registry of Deeds. In any event, a new lease on the home farm of Woodtown was signed in 1874 for the natural lives of Edward's sons Andrew and Edward and 'the survivor or survivors of them or for forty-one years whichever lasts longest subject to a yearly rent of £200 sterling.'[13] In 1870 Delany had bought the smaller of the two home farms, paying £2,700 for the 112 acres.[14]

In the context of grazing it is interesting to note some of the conditions of the 1874 lease. Delany was not permitted to plough any more than thirty Irish acres, anything above that would be subject to an additional yearly rent of £3 per acre. A second lease signed the same day on over 200 acres on land known as Brett's farm in Woodtown was subject to the same clause.[15] Such conditions were common at the time. An 1851 lease to another of the substantial farmers in the parish, John Daly of Cultromer, specified that Daly was not to 'plough into tillage or sow with any kind of grain, corn or hemp or flax' anything greater than forty Irish acres.[16] The fine in this case was £5 per acre over and above forty acres, at a time when the rental was less than £1 per acre. An 1878 lease involving 500 acres in Roestown and Leshemstown from Hans Hamilton Woods to James Maher allowed no more than sixty Irish acres to be in meadow in any year.[17] Even on a fifteen acre farm in Derrockstown the leasee was 'not to dig, plough, break or put under tillage more than 3a. 2r. 24p.' under penalty of an additional rent of £10 per acre.[18] Most of those leases also contained clauses preventing subletting without the landlord's consent, both conditions designed to keep the land as one holding and to ensure that they remained substantially in grass.

Delany's enterprise was based on the two farms in Woodtown, the home farm of 180 acres held on the lease referred to above, and 112 acres bought outright in 1870. From time to time he also leased extra land. Two of Delany's account books survive, one covering 1851 to 1879 and the second 1880 to 1899.[19] These detail his expenditure on buying and selling stock. He itemized each of the cattle he bought, recording the purchase price and often from whom it was bought, on the left hand columns, with the sale price directly opposite. He usually added in costs of travel and other expenses at fairs, yet he gave no details of other costs such as rent, fodder or wages. Even in the case of cattle which he stall fed over the winter there is only occasional reference to feeding costs. His chief concern was to calculate the gross margin between purchases and sales.

Delany's *modus operandi* shows little change over the half century. The main focus of his business was the annual buying and selling of up to 100 cattle for the Woodtown farms. He began stocking each year with a visit to the huge Ballinasloe fair in early October. He generally bought thirty cattle there and between the following March and May added up to eighty more. These were fattened during the summer and autumn and sold before the end of the year to be replaced by another set commencing in October. He supplemented this with small scale stall feeding over the winter. Invariably a dozen to twenty cattle were bought in November and sold by February, bringing in a profit of up to £100 in a good year. He also traded in sheep using the visit to Ballinasloe in October to buy up to 100 wethers which were sold the following May and June at profits which rarely amounted to more than £1 per head. In April just before the wethers were all sold, he bought in fifty hoggets on average which he fattened and sold off gradually from July to December, the sale of wool helping to boost his profits. There is no evidence of any tillage farming but it is likely that some meadow was cut and saved as hay for the winter feeding.

The only alteration to the pattern was the leasing of extra land for a number of years which necessitated extra purchases but no change in approach. He leased 250 acres in Derrockstown in the early 1850s and Griffith's Valuation records Edward Delany leasing 104 acres in Bedfanstown from a relative of his own landlord in Woodtown. As there is no reference to this land in his account books it may not have been the Edward from Woodtown. However, his brother Mark purchased it outright in 1870 on the same day Edward bought his 112 acres in Woodtown. He also leased land in Readsland in 1873, 1880, 1881, 1890 and 1891, probably 107 acres held by John Ball from Hans H. Woods. Ball was married to Edward's sister Mary and died in 1872.

Delany, it appears, bought most of the animals himself, travelling widely to do so. Taking the year 1868–69 at random, he bought thirty-three cattle in Ballinasloe on 9 October 1868. To complete his quota he bought again as follows, 1 April 1869 in Ratoath, 21 April in Tullow, 25 April in Moate, 3 May in Granard and 16 May in Strokestown.[20] To buy eighty-two animals for Readsland in 1890–91 he visited Loughrea, Strokestown (twice), Leitrim, Moate and Ballinasloe. On 7 April he bought sixty-eight hoggets in Mullingar and the stocking of Woodtown, now up to 500 acres with the addition of Brett's farm involved trips to the following towns with numbers purchased in brackets: Ballinasloe (30), Summerhill (1), Roscommon (20), Athlone (8), Kilkenny (10), Roscommon (29), Moate (18), Ballinasloe (20) and Galway (8) in that order.[21] For sales he rarely mentioned places, giving buyers' names usually, but it is clear many were sold in Dublin, while a number were sent to Liverpool or Manchester. He tended to sell in smaller lots than he bought, probably waiting until each animal was fully ready before selling it on.

In the nineteenth century transportation of animals obviously posed more problems than would be the case today. Padraig Colum's poem *The Drover* recalls the pre-railway days when he speaks of

> To Meath of the pastures
> From wet hills by the sea,
> Through Leitrim and Longford
> Go my cattle and me[22]

implying that cattle were driven long distances from fairs by drovers. Drovers still earned a living in Delany's day but his accounts begin when the railways were already extensive and he used rail transport for parts of the journeys. By 1848 the Midland and Great Western Railway operated a line from Dublin westwards through Enfield, Moyvalley and Hill of Down in County Meath. The line was extended to Ballinasloe and Galway in 1851.[23] A rail line from Dublin into Meath through Dunboyne, Batterstown, Drumree, Kilmessan and Navan was opened in 1863.[24] However, the latter was of little value if the grazier was bringing cattle from the west for they would have had to go to Dublin before switching to a Meath train. Accordingly it seems that Enfield or kilcock were the chief disembarkation points for the newly purchased animals of many Meath graziers, including Edward Delany. Kilcock was less than ten miles from Woodtown so it made sense to rail the animals to Kilcock and walk them home from there. Even into the late 1900s drovers were active on the roads. William Bulfin comments that along the roads between Trim and Westmeath, Meath ranchmen were trooping their store cattle from the fair of Ballinasloe and 'you will have to fight drovers at every two or three hundred yards of the road from Kilmessan to Ballivor.'[25] Sheep it seems were rarely walked, even from the railways, as they would not be physically capable of covering long distances. Thomas Leonard, another Dunshaughlin grazier, referred to floats waiting at Enfield to bring his newly purchased sheep to Warrenstown.[26]

The transportation of cattle by rail was not universally welcomed. A departmental committee appointed by the Board of Agriculture reported in 1898 on the issue.[27] There had been numerous complaints from butchers of unnecessary suffering and damage to animals carried by train, while farmers and traders were unhappy about delays and costs. Thomas Leonard, a son of Patrick Leonard who bought extensively in Culmullen in 1850 and who married into the Johnson family from Warrenstown where he farmed 1,000 acres, complained of delays and lack of supervision at railway stations. He gave as examples the presence of 'town roughs' who caused injuries while loading cattle. He also instanced buying sheep at Ballinasloe and having them at the railway station there by 9 a.m. for loading but due to the non-appearance of wagons they were not loaded until midday. The sheep did not arrive in Enfield until 3 to 4 a.m. the next morning where Leonard's men had been waiting since 3 p.m. the day before. Leonard claimed that the sheep suffered as a result of the delay.[28]

The railway line to Dublin was undoubtedly utilized by Dunshaughlin farmers like Delany, Leonard, the Dalys, Geraghtys, and others to take finished cattle into the Dublin market or on the first leg of the journey overseas. Drumree station was in the centre of the parish and Batterstown and Dunboyne stops were close at hand also. Batterstown and Drumree had long sidings to cater for loading and offloading animals and pens to corral them until collection or while awaiting the arrival of trains. However, Dublin victuallers were unanimous, the report said, that cattle walked into the Dublin market arrived in a better condition than those railed in, the latter often having injuries not visible until slaughter. Mr. W.P. Delaney of Dorset Street would pay up to 10s. more per animal for those walked in.[29] Patrick Leonard, a nephew of Thomas in Warrenstown, also gave examples of delays and injuries. He also stated that prior to the construction of the Meath-Dublin Railway the big Meath farmers had small farms all the way into Dublin and that they started out well in advance of the sale and stopped three to four days at each place. This information, he claimed came from his father.[30] It may well be that there was at least an informal network among graziers whereby those living long distances from Dublin could rest their animals at other graziers' farms along the way. At any rate it is clear that graziers in Dunshaughlin parish used trains but large numbers may still have been walked, particularly as the Dublin cattle market was situated on the north side of the city.

Having looked at the background of the graziers' operation the question which arises is how profitable the enterprise was. Figure 5 summarizes Delany's profits.[31] The most striking aspect of Delany's fortunes is their variability, with good years likely to be followed by bad and vice versa. Nevertheless a number of underlying trends are apparent. In general the period prior to 1876 is one of reasonable stability, profits tended, in the main, to rise and when drops occurred they were not severe. The period from 1876 was marked by much greater volatility, it contained both the best and the worst years of the accounts, 1882 and 1878 respectively.

The first period was one of steady progress. The 1860s were better overall than the 1850s and the best years were from 1864 until the late 1870s, 1869 being the best year of this span. Net profits ranged from a low of £170 in 1862 to a high of £512 in 1869. Throughout, Delany's costs showed a steady rise, up from £1,237 in 1852–53 to £2,563 in 1875–76, more than double. In the same period income from sales had jumped from £1,853 to £3,294 a 78 per cent increase. His gross profit showed a more modest increase of 18 per cent on the 1852–53 figure. Thus, although he was getting better prices for his stock he was also paying substantially more for them and accordingly risking more of his capital. On average Delany's purchases represented up to three quarters of his income from sales so that a large proportion of his income was

5. Edward Delany, Net Profits, *1853–99*

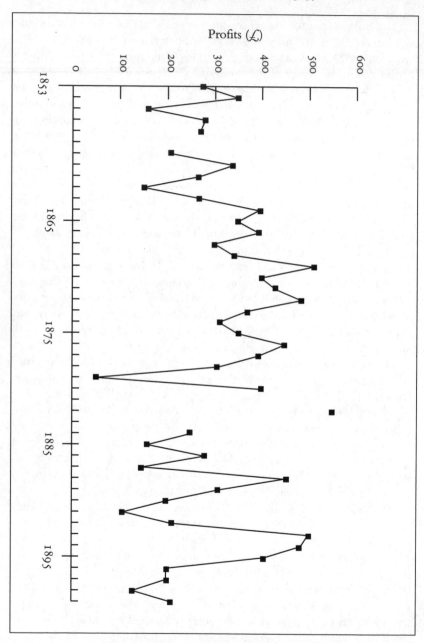

Source: Farm account books of Edward Delany, NLI MSS 19347–8.
For summary figures see Appendix 5.

constantly reinvested and at risk of loss in a bad year. His profits rarely represented more than 15 per cent of income from sales, so a rise in costs or a drop in income could have a dramatic effect on his profits. As an example of this, between 1854 and 1855 costs rose by 24 per cent while sales rose by just 8 per cent. Profits as a result were down from £343 to £176, effectively halved. In subsequent years costs dropped back, thereby enabling Delany to reestablish his more normal profit pattern. Certainly to prosper, Delany and his type needed to buy as cheaply as possible.

The period from 1876 to the end of the century was characterized by much greater volatility with buoyant years likely to be followed by sudden slumps. 1879 was a catastrophe for Delany with profits at their lowest ever as expenses were barely recouped while it was the third consecutive year of declining profits. He managed a mere gain of £31 on 160 sheep, about 4s. a head, compared to a normal profit nearer £1. On his major enterprise, cattle fattening at Woodtown, profits were down to £2 15s. a head on average instead of the normal £4 to £4. 10s.[32] Though the early 1880s brought a reversal of fortune the trend was soon downward again. From 1874 Delany held another 209 acres, Brett's farm, and from 1889 onwards the outgoings and profits on this farm are included in the profits given in Figure 5, as the accounts no longer distinguish between the farms. Delany's turnover therefore is much larger from 1889–90 but profits continued to swing violently over the final decade, continuing the pattern evident since the 1880s.

Over the full run of the accounts nevertheless Delany received a good return on his money. His profits as a proportion of expenditure gave him a return of almost 18 per cent in the first two decades, dropping to 14 per cent in the 1880s and 9 per cent in the final decade. (Table 6) Those figures do not allow for costs which Delany does not include in his accounts such as maintenance of farm and buildings, labour costs and winter feed. On the other hand, as Vaughan points out, his capital was not actually tied up for the whole year but recouped and reinvested during it.[33] Even if other costs reduced his return by a few percentage points he gained more than the normal return on money invested with the banks, which returned no more than 5 per cent.

Table 6. Delany's Profits as Proportion of expenditure.

Years	Average per cent Profit
1852–1860	18.6
1860–1870	18.6
1870–1880	16.1
1880–1890	14.5
1890–1899	9.2

Source: Calculations based on Farm account books of Edward Delany, NLI, MSS 19347–8.

Furthermore, profits on the Woodtown lands were not the only source of income available to Delany. From time to time he rented land in the vicinity, probably for eleven months and stocked it with the aim of making a quick profit. The benefit of such rentals can be seen in 1880. After his worst year on record he stocked Readsland with sixty-one cattle at a cost of £834 and made a profit of £300 and a further £46 on sheep. Allowing for a rent of £140, 30 per cent above the valuation, he still cleared £200. In 1890 he recorded £230 profit before deducting rent.[34]

The results of Delany's success as a grazier were to be seen in his gradual acquisition of more land in Woodtown. When the whole townland came up for sale as one lot in the Incumbered Estates Court in 1850 Delany was not among the bidders. It is unlikely he would have wanted or been able to pay the £3,450 it cost. Neither did he bid on any of the smaller lots available in the same sale in neighbouring townlands.[35] By 1870 however, he was obviously in a much stronger financial position and he purchased the 112 acres in Woodtown for £2,700, made up of £1,200 of his own money and £1,500 of a loan from the Commissioners of Public Works.[36] As the 1860s and 1870s had been among the most successful of his career he was obviously in a position to fund the £1,200 from his own resources. His accounts only rarely contain details of his assets but between 1856 and 1867 he kept some details which included cash, bank and railway shares and government stock. These show an increase in savings from £1,015 in 1856 to £2,265 in 1867, indicating annual savings of just over £100.[37]

Table 7. Landholders in Townlands of Woodtown, 1854–1911.

	1854		1911	
Name	*Area*	*Name*		*Area*
	a. r. p.			a. r. p.
Bridget Delany	112:2:21	William Delany		112:2:21
Philip Purdon	198:2:23	William Cooney		198:2:23
Andrew Sheridan	47:0:00	Thomas Sheridan		47:0:00
James Connell	99:1:33	William Delany		99:1:33
John P. Brett	209:0:39	Edward Delany		209:0:39
Edward Delany	179:3:39	Edward Delany		178:3:39
		Richard Lamb		1:0:00
Patrick Boylan	58:3:18	Owen Smith		58:3:18
Michael Byrne	14:2:12	Michael Smith		14:2:12
Anne Melady	26:3:24	Christopher Melady		26:3:24

Source: General valuation of rateable property in Ireland, Union of Dunshaughlin, valuation of the several tenements, (Dublin 1854) and Valuation Office, Cancelled land books.

In 1874 he added to his holding, leasing 209 acres known as Brett's Farm for forty-one years at £320 sterling per annum. He was also obliged to spend £160 within four years on draining, planting hedges and keeping the premises in repair.[38] Four years before he died he transferred his 112 acres in Woodtown to William his oldest son.[39] By 1911 the Delanys held or owned outright 600 of the 947 acres in the townland where in 1854 they held 292. This change is shown in Table 7.

The other noteworthy aspect of the townland is the degree of stability both in the size of the farms and the continuation of the names over the sixty years. Indeed the only alteration to the farm sizes was the reduction of Delany's farm by one acre which was acquired by the Rural District Council to provide a labourer's cottage.[40]

Graziers were often subject to disparaging remarks about their social pretensions and their efforts to ingratiate themselves with the gentry. Bulfin claimed that, with a few exceptions, 'the grazierocracy of Ireland was shoneen to the core.'[41] The majority of graziers in Dunshaughlin do not seem to have had aspirations to join the social elite but they certainly stood out from the labourers and the medium sized farmers and tended to marry their social equals. Delany refers in 1856 to his carriage and gig, a light two-wheeled one-horse carriage which would probably set him apart from most of his neighbours. Edward's own descriptions of himself varied. The 1901 census and the abstract of his will describes him as a 'farmer.'[42] When buying the 112 acres in 1870 he was a 'grazier' but a mere 'tenant farmer' when borrowing £95 for farm improvements from the Public Works Commissioners.[43] He only once described himself as a 'gentleman farmer.'[44]

Nevertheless if one looks at the position of the big farmers–cum–graziers using criteria like residence, wealth, political involvement it is clear that they formed the apex of local society in the late nineteenth century. There were forty farms of over 100 acres in the parish in the 1900s occupied by twenty-nine different individuals.[45] Of those twenty-nine, seventeen lived in or near the area with twelve defined as absent. While the homes of those seventeen did not match those of the landed gentry they stood apart from other houses in the locality. All occupied first or second class houses according to the 1901 Census. Only two had thatch roofs, Mulvany in Ballinlough and Daly in Cultromer, all had stone walls and the majority had six rooms or more. All boasted extensive outoffices, usually over ten, combining stables, cowhouses, calf sheds etc. Edmund Morris in Gaulstown (Dunshaughlin), a farmer and horse breeder, had thirty while Thomas Leonard in Warrenstown (Knockmark) had thirty-two. The valuation of the buildings averaged £6. 10s., if one excludes Leonard's mansion and buildings which were rated at £51.10s. Edward Delany's home in 1911 was a second class house with eight rooms, by 1911 it had ten rooms and was rated first class and had fourteen outoffices attached.

Many employed servants, but to a modest degree, usually one or two. Edward Delany, his son and daughter had one domestic servant. Edmund Morris and his wife in Gaulstown had two, even though they had no family, while the Geraghtys in Merrywell had three, two domestic and a farm servant. Thomas Leonard and his wife Annette lived in the grand manner with a butler, cook, two housemaids and a coachman to attend to their needs.[46] By 1911 the coachman had disappeared as they had purchased a motor-car and Thomas described himself as a 'gentleman farmer.'[47] Few wills survive but Thomas Murphy's of Dunshaughlin, dated 1883, gives some indication of the wealth and status of the better-off farmer. He bequeathed to his wife Rose Anne, 'all my furniture, plate, plated articles, linen, china, glass, wines, liquors, consumable stores, and articles of household and domestic use and ornament.' He also left her an annuity of £100 to be paid out of 'my leasehold farm' of 102 Irish acres in Derrockstown. The farm went to his nephew Thomas Angelo. To his nephew John he left 'my leasehold farm and lands of Johnstown containing 120 acres' and to another nephew Patrick a leasehold farm of seventy Irish acres in Cooksland and ninety acres in Rathhill. The leasehold house in Dunshaughlin was left to his widow and another house 'at present set' to an R.I.C. man was intended for Patrick. In addition to this he refers to 'the rest residue and remainder of my property including debts due to me, cattle, sheep, horses, stock and effects.'[48] Clearly a man of some substance.

In an era when there was no widows' pension those who could afford to usually provided for their wife in their will as above, or often prior to marriage. The latter was a characteristic of marriages among the upper classes but it was emulated by some of the strong farmers. In the 1870s Hugh Geraghty received a marriage portion of £500 from his future wife Margaret McCormack and in return it was agreed that he should settle a jointure of £50 on Margaret in the event of her surviving him, chargeable on the lands and premises.[49] James Geraghty also received £500 prior to his marriage to Catherine Dunne which was to be invested in government stock for her future benefit.[50] Mark Delany who bought Bedfanstown in 1870, but who lived in Navan, also placed a charge on those lands to provide £100 per annum for his wife Mary Ann Cullen in case of his death.[51]

Many of the substantial farmers were related through marriage. Edward Delany's sister Mary married John Ball, who held 107 acres in Readsland, the land Edward took for grazing towards the end of the century. Edward's brother Mark and his (Edward's) son William married the Cullen sisters of Liscarton, Navan. The Cullens held almost 750 acres there and the girls were nieces of Cardinal Paul Cullen. An uncle of the Cullens, Hugh Cullen, who was a cattle salesmaster, a government adviser on the cattle trade and a director of the Bank of Liverpool, married Elizabeth Leonard, daughter of Patrick Leonard who purchased land in Culmullen in 1850. (See Chapter 2). As previously noted Thomas Leonard married Annette Johnson, the owner of over 1,000 acres in Knockmark and Warrenstown. Edward Delany's own wife's family, the Barrys, held 229 acres in Cookstown within five miles of Woodtown and Thomas Delany's family in Dunshaughlin was related to the Murphy and the Morris families, both of whom were also extensive landholders.[52] More extensive research would probably reveal further interrelationships between the families; it seems that marriage outside their social equals was rare.

A number of those farmers involved themselves in local politics mainly at poor law union level.[53] Edward Delany served as a Poor Law Guardian, a tradition carried on by his son Edward, while Patrick Mulvany became active in local politics in the 1900s serving as chairman of Dunshaughlin rural district council and as Meath county councillor. He was also active in the United Irish League and he later became a T.D. in the 1920s for the short lived Irish Farmers' Party. Mark Delany and Edmund Morris were both justices of the peace. Tom Leonard's and Edward Kelly's wives were also members of the R.D.C. The Kellys lived just outside the parish in Crackenstown but held almost 500 acres in Bonestown and Thomastown from Thomas E. Taylor. A number seem to have involved themselves in politics at the time of the Parnell controversy but to have opted out later. In the Poor Law Union elections of 1893 Edmund Morris and an E. Delany were elected in Dunshaughlin, standing as Nationalists, while John Morrin and Hugh Geraghty stood unsuccessfully as Parnellites. In the Culmullen division Edward Delany topped the poll for the Nationalists while Michael Byrne with 130 acres in Curraghtown finished second and was the only Parnellite elected in the parish.[54]

Of the large landholders the most prominent were the Leonards. The family held extensive lands in Macetown in the neighbouring parish of Skryne in the 1790s and continued to farm there during the following century. In evidence given to the committee investigating the transport of cattle in 1898 Patrick Leonard, junior, explained that the firm of Leonard and Son of Dublin and Liverpool had been in business since 1800 trading from father to son.[55] It is likely that those involved were Patrick (1785–1861) who bought the lands in Culmullen-Curraghtown in 1850 and Pelletstown in 1858, his son John (1829–1896) and his grandson Patrick, junior (1861–1944) who appeared before the committee. A brother of Patrick junior, John junior (1866–1946) was also involved as a cattle salesmaster and he owned the Culmullen lands at the end of the century. He lived in Dublin and seems to have entrusted the farm in Culmullen to a steward or herd, eventually coming to live in Culmullen in 1917 and buying more land there.[56] Patrick junior told the cattle transit committee that he managed for clients and worked for his own profit and loss 3,000 acres in Meath, Kildare and Dublin. One of those farms was in Warrenstown (Culmullen) where he held 250 acres at the turn of the century. Both the older John and Patrick were J.Ps. while John junior later became a member of Meath County Council.

Thomas Leonard of Warrenstown in Knockmark (1841–1920) was a brother of John senior. He was also a salesmaster, with the family firm initially and later with Leonard and Aungier. He came into possession of the Warrenstown lands by marrying Annette Johnson in 1874. The Johnsons were descendants of the Warrens who gave their name to the townland and they were the biggest landholders in the parish. Thomas informed the cattle transit committee that his chief business was cattle rearing. He stated that he bought stores in the west and south selling most of them fat, usually in the Dublin market.[57] Reference has already been made to his household and mansion with a tenement valuation of £51.10s., by far the most valuable in the whole parish. He was a magistrate, a member of the county grand jury and deputy lieutenant for County Meath and his wife Annette served on the local Rural Council up to 1907.

Those various families, then, were the elite of the parish during the nineteenth and early twentieth centuries. If Delany's account books are any guide they prospered up to 1880 with the later years marked by fluctuating fortunes when profitable grazing required a combination of good luck and good judgement. It seems that much more land came on the market for letting annually in the latter period, suggesting that more profit was to be had by setting the land for eleven months than risking investment in stock.[58] However the demand for such land implies that for those with capital it was still a worthwhile venture. Delany's returns would substantiate this. The success of graziers was evident in the acquisition of extra land by men like Delany, the Geraghtys and Dalys and the quality of their residences. Even in death their status is manifest. Edward Delany's monument in Culmullen cemetery is a substantial stone and concrete structure, 3.6m high topped by a Celtic cross. It is the tallest and most imposing structure in the cemetery. Thomas Leonard had an equally striking monument erected in Knockmark cemetery with a huge Celtic Cross on top of a substantial base. The cross with intricate carving on all four sides has an 80cm diameter.

However the new century brought many challenges to the graziers' position as the tenants and labourers pressed for more of a share in the land of Meath. The next chapter considers their position.

Agricultural Labourers and Farmers,
1854–1911

Families like the Delanys and Leonards represented those at the apex of the farming community but the majority of landholders in the parish survived on smaller holdings. Twenty per cent of all farms were in the fifteen to 100 acre range and another third were from one to fifteen acres.[1] In addition there was a substantial number of landless labourers. Evidence on the situation of the medium sized landholders is much more difficult to come by than information on the substantial farmers as they left few records. Nevertheless, through the use of valuation office records, deeds and census returns it is possible to assess their position in the community and arrive at some conclusions, albeit tentative. It has already been noted in the second chapter that the major landholders held 59 per cent of the land in the parish. Holdings between fifteen and 100 acres accounted for another 4,356 acres in 1854, 31 per cent of the total. Thus between them both groups accounted for 90 per cent of all the land in the rural parish.

A comparison of Griffith's Valuation as printed in 1854 with the revised valuation books c.1910 enables one to plot changes in farm sizes and occupancy among those on fifteen to 100 acres. The most notable finding to emerge is one which parallels to some extent the findings for the major landholders, that the number and size of such farms remained very stable, while 45 per cent of farms remained with the same family over the half century. Ninety-three such individual farms were identified for 1854. However, a detailed examination of those reveals that matters are more complex as a number of people owned two or more farms in this category. Excluding those who had a combined acreage in excess of 100 acres the number of people actually farming between fifteen and 100 acres was sixty-eight.

Sixty years later the number was practically the same at sixty-five. In the intervening period only two of the large farms had been subdivided, 116 acres in Gaulstown (Culmullen) had been broken into four smaller holdings while 188 acres in Barstown produced two farms of ninety-five and ninety-three acres. Derrockstown also gained two farms. However those increases were negated by consolidation of other farms with the Delanys of Dunshaughlin and the Maddens and Rourkes in Augherskea expanding their acreages.[2]

An examination of the individual farms shows only minimal change in extent over the sixty years. Many remained intact to the perch and often such change as took place was accounted for by the building of a labourer's cottage on the land. Table 7 in the previous chapter shows the degree of continuity in Woodtown and a similar situation is found in many other townlands. In Dunshaughlin townland there were nine holdings between fifteen and 100 acres in 1854, only two of them changed in size between then and 1910, the other seven remaining precisely the same. In Augherskea, out of twelve farms only two underwent even marginal change in size.

There is also a substantial degree of continuity in family occupancy of the farms. In twenty-nine of the sixty-five farms the surname didn't change, the farm remaining in the same family over the period. It is likely that in a few other cases a female inherited and the farm was recorded in her husband's name on marriage so the figure of twenty-nine, equivalent to 45 per cent, may underestimate the degree of continuity and stability. Most of the changes occurred in townlands where auctions were held under the various Incumbered Estates Acts which usually brought a new owner. This was so in Derrockstown with four, and Pelletstown and Culmullen with two auctions each. Overall, Culmullen civil parish experienced most change, due probably to the number of townlands where sales took place. However, even in townlands subject to sales there is often continuity, suggesting that many Incumbered Estates buyers retained the existing tenants. Table 8 shows the extent of continuity in Augherskea and Dunshaughlin townlands.[3]

Not all townlands displayed the degree of continuity revealed here and the scale of change was certainly greater in those medium sized farms than on the substantial farms discussed in the previous chapter. However, an overall figure of up to 50 per cent of farms remaining in the same family is high during a period noted for turmoil on the land question. Families like the Rourkes, Maddens, Mooneys and Wildridges in Augherskea, the Coffeys in Kilcooley, the Tyrrells and Sheridans in Baltrasna, the Marmions and Lawlesses in Bogganstown and Woodcockstown, the Rices in Gaulstown (Culmullen), among others, remained from the 1850s to 1910, and in many cases beyond.

Some of the farms in this category were close in size to those of the major landholders considered in the last chapter and given the proportion of the whole Union under grass by the turn of the century there is every reason for assuming that grazing was practised extensively on those farms also. There is some evidence to support this. A lease for Patrick Mullen's forty-four acres in Dunshaughlin describes Mullen as a 'hotel keeper and grazier' and Thomas Delany, who bought Mullen's interest in the lease, as a 'grazier'.[4] Roll books from the National Schools in Dunshaughlin describe a number of families as graziers, for example the Delanys in Rathill in 1867 and 1870, the Everards of Gaulstown (Dunshaughlin) as well as the substantial landholders like the Morrins and Murphys of Dunshaughlin. Indeed, many whom we know to be graziers such as the Woodtown Delanys are recorded as farmers in the roll books and it is likely that the teacher recording the details did not always

Table 8. Continuity and change in Farm size and occupancy in two Townlands, 1854–*c*.1911.

1854			*c*.1911		
		Augherskea			
Occupier	Lessor	Extent	Occupier	Lessor	Extent
Mgt. Gearty	Oliver Cranmer	67:3:35	Mgt. Gearty	In fee	68:0:35
Mary Rourke	Oliver Cranmer	15:2:02	Mary Kennedy	John Tisdall	15:2:02
Jas. Wildridge	Oliver Cranmer	20:0:13	Thos Wildridge	John Tisdall	15:2:02
Hugh Rourke	Henry White	97:0:11	Mary Rourke	In fee	95:2:00
Mary Rourke	Henry White	45:2:06	Bridget Rourke	In fee	45:2:06
Ml. Rourke	Henry White	28:1:04	Wm. Rourke	In fee	28:1:04
Nicl. Rourke jn.	Henry White	46:3:17	Bridget Rouke	In fee	46:3:17
Nicl. Rourke	Henry White	60:2:05	Bridget Rourke	In fee	62:1:10
Ml. Madden	Henry White	83:2:02	John Madden	In fee	83:2:02
Wm. Madden	Henry White	50:2:25	Thomas Quinn	In fee	50:2:25
Wm. Murphy	Henry White	36:0:20	John Madden	In fee	36:0:20
John Mooney	Henry White	41:2:24	Robert Mooney	In fee	42:0:14
		Dunshaughlin			
Chris. Murphy	Will. Bond	34:2:13	Peter Moran	Imm. lessor	34:2:13
Rch. Barnewall	Patk. Barnewall	60:0:18	Chris. Tallon	La Nauze trust	60:0:18
Thos. Kellett	La Nauze trust	43:3:01	John Kellett	La Nauze trust	43:3:01
Andrew Moore	E.H. Casey	25:3:02	Bridget Moore	E.H. Casey	25:3:02
David Supple	In fee	18:1:12	Chris Tallon	W.R. Supple	18:1:02
Wm. Murphy	Fredk. Supple	53:2:32	Patk. Murphy	F.A. Supple	63:1:08
Wm. Murphy	Fredk. Supple	42:0:14	Patk. Murphy	La. Nauze trust	34:1:00
Patk Mullen	Fredk. Supple	44:0:22	Thos. Delany	F.A. Supple	44:0:22
Catherine Day	Walter Nugent	54:3:28	Thos. Delany	Walter Nugent	54:3:28

Note: only medium sizes farms in the respective townlands are included here.
Source: General valuation of rateable property in Ireland, Union of Dunshaughlin, valuation of the several tenements, (Dublin 1854) and Valuation Office, Revised valuation books.

distinguish graziers from farmers.[5] Newspaper advertisements also indicate the prevalence of grazing on those medium sized farms.[6] This does not mean that tillage was non-existent, especially in the early years as will be seen later, but it was a declining form of livelihood in the community.

Many of those occupiers held their land on medium term leases. As many families remained in occupation throughout the period under review they were obviously reliable tenants, capable of paying their rent and probably making a reasonable living. Leases varied, with twenty-one or thirty-one years the most common. Henry White, Baron Annaly, signed ten leases in 1862–63 with his tenants in Augherskea almost all for twenty-one years with rents averaging £1. 4s. per acre. Among the inducements to prospective buyers when the farms came up for sale in 1867 was the fact that 'the tenants have good interests, and pay their rents punctually'.[7] Such a remark may contain estate agents' hyperbole but there is more than a grain of truth in it given the lack of turnover among the tenants in the townland. He also gave a mixture of twenty-one and thirty-one year leases in Warrenstown (Culmullen) and Woodcockstown.[8] Most of Samuel Dopping's land in Culmullen and Curraghtown which was sold in 1850 had tenants with leases of thirty-one years or three lives, dating from the late 1820s.[9] The farms in Woodtown also had leases for thirty-one or forty-one years.[10] Thus, tenants who could continue to pay their rents had reasonable security of tenure. The ability of the large tenant such as Edward Delany or the Geraghtys to buy land in the 1870s has been noted. Some medium sized tenants were obviously prospering also, for J.G. Carleton, with eighty-seven acres in Culmullen, was able to bid £1,200 for a lot containing his rented farm when it was auctioned in 1850. However, he was unable to match higher bids.[11] Whereas the majority of the big farmers may have been able to weather agricultural recessions it is likely that those on smaller holdings were more vulnerable. Evidence for this is scanty however. The Land League seems to have had little impact on the area and there is very little evidence of boycotting.[12] A number of tenants did avail of provisions in the 1881 Land Act which gave power to Civil Bill Courts to fix a fair or judicial rent. A number of notices entitled Notices to Fix Fair Rents under the act have survived for County Meath, almost 1,000 in all from 1882 to 1890, the vast majority referring to estates in the north of the county.[13] Only about thirty concern Dunshaughlin. These refer in the main to Augherskea and Pelletstown, townlands consisting primarily of medium sized holdings. Cases referred to the court almost always resulted in a judicial rent lower than the actual rent, with the reduction varying from 20 per cent up to the low thirties. The overall effect was to bring the judicial rent close to the poor law valuation, most judgements ranged between 10 per cent above or below it. A number of reductions were by agreement and given that reductions between a quarter and a third were achieved it is surprising more tenants didn't avail of the legislation. It is possible that some may have come to private agreements and another may be that non-resident graziers were excluded from its benefits, initially at least.[14] An examination of a number of tenants who had judicial rents fixed reinforces the impression of continuity and stability already referred to. One such tenant was Thomas Quinn. He had fifty acres with a poor law valuation of £41 for which he paid £62. 10s. The rent was reduced to £41 which represented a reduction of 34.4 per cent. Quinn held the land from the 1880s but the rent had been fixed at £62. 10s. by an 1863 lease between the previous occupant and Baron Annaly. Mary Madden's holding of eighty-three acres with a rental of £101. 16s. 4d. and a poor law valuation of £82 was reduced to £80. This farm was held by the Maddens from at least 1863 without any change in rental. Both Quinn and Madden held their land in fee by the 1900s.

On a smaller scale Stephen Dowdall held twenty-two acres in Pelletstown valued at £18. 15s. for which he paid £27. 12s. rent by an 1879 lease. This was reduced to £19, a fall of 31 per cent. The Kevlins held twenty acres (and a public house) in Warrenstown (Culmullen) at £28. 15s. on an 1863 lease which was reduced to £22 by consent.[15] By 1910 the Kevlins were still in possession and the Dowdall farm was held by Francis Kelly, a nephew of the Dowdalls.

The evidence implies that the medium sized land holders were a relatively stable element in the rural landscape, many of whom retained their farms throughout the period under review. A number availed of the opportunity to benefit from rent reductions in the 1880s. Reductions were so large due to the severe agricultural depression of the mid 1880s and in many parts of the country even judicial rents were too high for the poorer smaller tenants.[16] As extensive graziers like Edward Delany experienced substantial drops in income in this period many of his medium sized neighbours must have suffered financial difficulties also, but obviously the majority survived the recession and many became owners of their farms in the early part of the new century.

The farmer on fifteen to 100 acres did not have the same standard of housing as the substantial farmer. In 1854 the rateable valuation of the majority of residences and outbuildings was between £1 and £2 with very few over £4. By the 1900s many had improved. Among those referred to earlier Dowdalls of Pelletstown went from £2 to £5. 5s., Maddens in Augherskea from £2 to £4, Kevlins from £2 to £7. 10s. and Quinn remained on £1. 10s. In the 1901 census the houses on those four farms were rated second class, first class, second class and third class respectively and in general farmers who were not in the big farming class had second and third class residences.[17]

It is not possible to say why farms which did not remain with the same family changed hands. A change of owner under a Landed Estates' Court sale may have been one cause although not all townlands experienced a turnover of tenants in such situations. The 1901 census returns suggest another possible cause. It reveals that a high proportion of the heads of families were unmarried and if this characteristic held true for the preceding decades, then in many cases, there may not have been a family member to inherit on the death of the tenant or the farm may have passed to a relation with a different surname. Detailed genealogical investigation would be necessary to make definitive statements on the issue.

In the rural landscape the landless labourers were at the bottom of the pyramid along with those on small non-viable holdings of an acre or less. They exist as mere statistics from the nineteenth century, little evidence remains of their homes, lifestyle or material culture and it is accordingly very difficult to reconstruct and assess their role in the farming community. Nevertheless, an analysis of the available evidence sheds valuable light on their position and status.

Griffith's Valuation of 1854 shows that while the substantial and medium sized farmers monopolized the land of the parish they were eclipsed numerically by occupants of holdings consisting of a house with no land attached or holdings of less than an acre. Almost 25 per cent of dwellings belonged to the former category and another 8 per cent to the latter, though not all contained houses. (Table 2). An analysis of the valuation in 1854 and comparison with the revised valuation in the 1900s leads to two conclusions; firstly, that such landless labourers were not evenly spread over the townlands but were concentrated in some and totally absent in others and secondly, that large numbers of them disappeared from the parish over the half century.

In 1854 a number of townlands were totally devoid of landless homes or houses on less than an acre. These were almost always townlands dominated by one or more large farms. The biggest townland, Culmullen had six farms over 100 acres, including one of 343 acres, but only one landless cottage. The second largest townland, Woodtown had four farms over 100 acres and no landless cottage. This was a pattern repeated in Ballinlough, Ballymurphy, both Gaulstowns, Johnstown, Thomastown, Hayestown and Warrenstown (Knockmark).

In the rural parish as a whole there were 148 houses on plots of less than one acre in 1854 and they were concentrated in a few townlands. Each of the following had five or more, Dunshaughlin and Augherskea sixteen each, Curraghtown and Cultromer nine each, Grangend eight, Barstown, Pelletstown and Readsland six each and Redbog and Roestown five each, accounting for 53 per cent of all such houses. Many of those were near the town of Dunshaughlin, but a number especially Augherskea, Curraghtown, Cultromer and Pelletstown were in the rural heartland. Examples of the holders of substantial farms subletting plots are rare and as was noted in the previous chapter many leases specifically precluded such practices. Instead, those small landless cabins or homes on less than an acre were sublet from two sources: the medium sized landholders and from occupiers who themselves has very little land.

The best examples of the former occur in Augherskea, a townland dominated by the Rourkes. Hugh had ninety-seven acres in two sections and he sublet seven plots of less than an acre. Mary Rourke with sixty acres in three lots sublet five small plots.[18] In Cultromer, Christopher Geraghty with fifty-four acres had four subtenants with a house and no land attached while in Pelletstown a number of medium sized farmers had sublet one or more small parcels for housing.[19] A possible explanation for this is that tillage farming had not declined in the 1850s to the extent it did later in the century so a quota of regular labourers was required. This is implied in an advertisement for the sale of stock and implements on Michael Johnston's farm in Pelletstown in 1859. He was a substantial farmer whose land was purchased by Patrick Leonard who probably intended using it as another grazing farm. In addition to cattle and horses the inventory contained twelve stacks of oats, two of wheat and upwards of 100 barrels of potatoes with two iron ploughs and harrows.[20] He had sublet two pieces of land, one for a house without land and another of four acres and it is likely that both subtenants worked as labourers on his farm, given the evidence for tillage in the auction prospectus.[21]

However, the majority of landless labourers homes seem to have been sublet from people who themselves had only small holdings. Michael Hyland on seventeen acres in Merrywell sublet five small plots, Michael Gaffney with ten acres in Rathhill sublet two. In Grangend, nearer the town, Margaret Gelshenan had half an acre but sublet space for two cabins while Patrick Flynn on over an acre sublet space for one. Roestown provides an example of the complex system of subletting which could exist. Bridget Begg had almost fifty acres here in six separate parcels from the head landlord Hans H. Woods. She sublet six acres to a Patrick Daly, another six to James Meehan who in turn sublet to Thomas Meehan and Thomas in turn sublet to Mary Meehan! Begg also let four acres to Anne Corcoran and almost two acres to Patrick Reilly who sublet a cabin to Mary Reilly.[22]

Obviously many of those holdings were completely non-viable as farms and the occupants were dependant for employment on the larger farms. Such opportunities declined as grazing came to dominate the parish and the revised valuation books for the 1900s show that many of the landless occupants and those on less than an acre disappeared. Whereas 148 were identified in 1854 only sixty-six could be picked out fifty years later. This represents a decline of 55 per cent, a stark contrast to the stability and continuity noted among the substantial and medium farmers. The declines were in those townlands identified earlier as having large concentrations of landless persons in 1854. The total of all houses in Augherskea dropped from thirty-six to twenty-one, Curraghtown from twenty-one to twelve, Dunshaughlin twenty-four to ten, Pelletstown nineteen to twelve, Readsland ten to three and Redbog twenty-four to eleven. Analysis of the individual entries shows that most of those declines were due to the disappearance of houses on an acre or less, all of Readsland's decline of seven fell into this category, as did twelve of Augherskea's fifteen, five of Curraghtown's nine and eight of Redbog's thirteen.[23]

It is not clear what happened to those who disappeared. There is no evidence of any deliberate evictions and little comment on the gradual clearances until after 1900. Given the proximity to Dublin it is likely that many who left went there. The 1901 census remarks in connection with a population decline in Grangend between 1881 and 1901 that 'the decrease was attributed to emigration'.[24] Undoubtedly a number became homeless and the increase in the number of 'tramps' calling weekly to Dunshaughlin workhouse would add weight to this possibility although the workhouse catered for a much wider area than Dunshaughlin parish.[25] In the absence of concrete evidence it is not possible to draw authoritative conclusions.

The standard of housing endured by the landless was very low, with many no better than cabins. In 1854, 35 per cent of them were valued at 5s. or less and only 20 per cent were rated above 10s. Those in Culmullen civil parish were uniformly poor with 85 per cent of them rated below 5s.[26] Giving evidence to a select committee in 1871 the Roman Catholic bishop of Meath Dr. Nulty described the state of labourers in Westmeath as 'most deplorable'. He claimed that matters were even worse in Meath where 'they cut down bushes and trees where they are allowed to do so, and that is the only thing they have for fuel, so that their cabins and hovels in Meath are in a most wretched condition'.[27]

The 1901 census suggests some improvement in housing for those labourers who remained. Out of sixty-eight heads of household in the rural area engaged in agricultural labour thirty lived in second class houses, thirty-one in third class with the rest in fourth class accommodation.[28] Thus, just less than half were in second class housing. The reasons for the improvement were twofold. Firstly, the majority of those who left between 1854 and 1900 had occupied poorer class cabins. Secondly, various Labourers' Acts were passed beginning in 1883 which provided for the erection of labourers' cottages by the local board of guardians and from 1898 the rural district councils.[29] By 1895 140 had been built in the Dunshaughlin union while other Meath unions were even more active.[30] To quote the 1911 census the accommodation provided was a type with 'the character of good farm houses'.[31] An analysis of the revised valuation books reveals that about thirty-three were built in Dunshaughlin parish by 1910, although not without some opposition as will be seen in the next chapter.

It is not a simple matter to assess the earnings of labourers for, as David Fitzpatrick has stated, 'no data is so treacherous as that relating to agricultural wages.'[32] An 1870 report gives wages in Dunshaughlin union as 1s. 6d. per day or 8s. per week which was reckoned to represent an increase of 50 per cent over the previous twenty years, but labourers were described as 'not contented'. Other Meath unions were reported at 7s. weekly[33] and Bishop Nulty claimed a man would be 'content if he had 1s. a day.'[34] The reports of the Royal Commission on Labour in 1893 gave detailed accounts of a selection of unions. It quotes 8s. to 9s. weekly, with a few on 10s., for men in regular summer employment in Delvin, a union with a high incidence of grazing farms.[35] The 1901 agricultural returns for the Dunshaughlin constabulary district report daily rates from 2s. 6d. to 3s. for men in summer and 1s. 6d. to 1s. 8d. in winter, noting that 'the general wage for men is 10s. per week' while there is little employment for women as agricultural labourers.[36] The following year the figures are 3s. to 3s. 6d. in summer and 2s. to 2s. 6d. in winter.[37] Rates in the Dunshaughlin union were usually higher than in other Meath unions and indeed the 1902 figures are among the highest in the country. By the early

1900s there were many complaints of a scarcity of labourers, the 1901 census stating that 'there are fewer agricultural labourers in the country and those who are left are said to be not the most efficient.' It claims that as 'labour is scarce and dear' there is continuing trend towards grazing.[38] The 1893 Commission on Labour implies that the best labourers tended to emigrate.[39] In view of the persistent decline in the number of labourers in Dunshaughlin a scarcity of labour would not be surprising, for while tillage occupied but a small portion of Meath farmland by 1901 even small acreages required labour in the absence of mechanization. Even on grazing enterprises cutting and saving hay necessitated labour in summer and at least one of the substantial farmers, Edward Kelly, made silage from his meadows in 1896 which would have been labour intensive over a short term.[40] Nevertheless, one statistic which emphasizes the decline of the labourer in the parish is the farmer-labourer ratio. The 1831 census returns produce a ratio of 540 labourers per 100 farmers, by 1901 this was 237 to 100, a reduction of over 50 per cent.[41] Herds were usually better off than the general labourer. They had all year round employment, often had a herd's house on the land and a small garden and in some cases sufficient grass given free or at reduced rent for an animal or two. An employer in Delvin claimed that 'socially the herds considered themselves above the ordinary labourers.'[42] The role of the herd has been touched upon in the last chapter and in the 1900s there were thirty-four herds' houses in Dunshaughlin parish.[43]

This chapter has detailed the contrasts between the medium sized farmers and the agricultural labourer. Whereas the former, like the substantial farmers, were in the main a stable, relatively prosperous group, tending to stay in the parish over time, the labouring population suffered a huge drop in numbers. Much of this decline was attributable to the prevalence of grazing farms in the area and the consequent scarcity of labouring work. The new century would bring complaints about depopulation, demands for its reversal and reallocation of the land and pressure on the graziers to change their method of farming. The final chapter will consider those issues.

A Decade of Conflict, 1904–10

Population decline continued relentlessly during the second half of the nineteenth century. By 1901 the population of Dunshaughlin parish represented slightly over one half its 1851 figure. Excluding the town, and taking the rural part only, the figure was down from 2,025 to 940, representing 46 per cent of the 1851 total.[1] This decline continued over the next decade. Demographic decline was a national phenomenon in the nineteenth century but decreases of this magnitude were above the national average and even slightly higher than in many western areas. By 1901 Meath had the lowest number of inhabitants per square mile of arable land in the whole country, at seventy-four persons.[2] The Dunshaughlin union fell even below this, at 55.8.[3]

The level of depopulation was now so glaring that it dominated political rhetoric and public comment. Bernard Carolan's description of Dunshaughlin as a howling wilderness has already been noted. Such images were the common currency of nationalist political speeches at the turn of the century. Laurence Ginnell, M.P. for Westmeath, told Kells Rural District Council the people there were fortunate compared to Dunshaughlin as Kells contained 'some bad land, on which because it was bad, the people had been allowed to remain. If the land were good the people would have been wiped off it as they have been off the plain from Trim to Dublin.'[4]

An editorial in the nationalist *Drogheda Independent* declared that such areas are 'little better than vast deserts … of green grass on which there are no inhabitants of the human species, the magnificent fertility being given over to flocks and herds.'[5] William Bulfin's writings about Meath evince a sentimental nostalgic vision of 'pre grazier days' with 'homely sounds from the barn door … white-washed walls' and 'blue wreaths of turf smoke'. Now all was silence, 'a lovely wilderness of grass – a verdant fertile desert from which man had banished himself, and into which he had sent the beasts to take his place.'[6] The 1901 census returns for the parish reflect this sense of a vacant landscape, a number of townlands had no houses while twenty of them had a maximum of two each. The returns also show a number of imbalances in the population. In the eighteen to forty age group there were almost twice as many unmarried males as females, 212 as against 116 and the percentage of unmarried agricultural labourers over thirty years was very high at 65 per cent. Obviously chances of finding a marriage partner within the parish or town were limited for men. Farmers over thirty years of age, whose employment and residence was much more secure than the labourers, fared better in terms of marriage with 26 per cent of this occupational group unmarried.[7]

An important factor in determining population levels is the proportion of the population which married and the age on marriage. Jones has shown that in many districts of Meath and Westmeath over 25 per cent of the male population of fifty-five and above remained unmarried; for females of forty-five years or older the figure was slightly less.[8] Males over fifty-five had poor prospects of marriage while women over forty-five, even if they were to marry, were unlikely to bear children. In Dunshaughlin parish 28 per cent of the males over fifty-five and 22 per cent of females over forty-five were unmarried. All of those features of the population contributed to the decline in numbers and they portray a far from vibrant community.

Demands for the subdivison of large grazing farms among the smallholders began to increase around the turn of the century but particularly after the Wyndham Land Act of 1903. The agitation was most widespread in the west where there were large numbers of small non-viable farms alongside large grazing ranches and it was spearheaded by the United Irish League. The instigator-in-chief of the anti-grazier movement in the eastern counties was Laurence Ginnell, M.P. for North Westmeath from 1906 to 1918, whose forceful language and actions often went beyond what his party deemed politically acceptable. He was supported by David Sheehy, M.P. for South Meath 1903–18, a constituency which included Dunshaughlin. Sheehy had a chequered career, representing Galway South from 1885 to 1900 and spending some time in prison for his role in the Plan of Campaign.[9]

The main focus of concern was the letting of land on the eleven month system whereby holdings were let, usually by auction, to the highest bidder for eleven months, after which the land was again let. Eleven months was the preferred term as the occupier could not claim any formal tenancy or legal rights, a twelve month tenancy was necessary for this.[10] A witness to a select committee in 1871 claimed that the eleven month system was a Meath habit for many years 'but it has increased lately.'[11] As was noted in the fourth chapter Edward Delany was taking extra land, probably on this system, in Readsland in 1870 while in 1885 up to 600 acres in Culmullen were let to graziers.[12] Such lettings became increasingly popular towards the end of the century and had a number of advantages for the owner. As no formal tenancy was created they were not subject to the provisions of various land acts such as fair or judicial rents and it was much easier to obtain the rent from one well-off farmer than from a group of poorer tenants.

Those opposed to the eleven month system based their complaints on two factors. Firstly, by paying high prices for such land graziers were seen to be buttressing the position of the landlords and making them less likely to sell their land under the land acts. Bernard Carolan, at a meeting in Dunshaughlin stated that many of the local big farmers 'developed into grass grabbers and

the grass grabber as eleven month man is the only obstacle to the sale of numerous estates.'[13] Secondly, the continued expansion of grazing led to decreasing
employment opportunities for the labourer. The Meath Labour Union in 1907
wanted the county council to use agricultural labourers on the county roads
during the winter 'as there is no other employment to be found on the fertile
lands of Meath.' David Sheehy agreed, stating that 'these cattle ranches and the
abominable eleven months' system has been a curse to them [the labourers].'[14]

Such views led to an anti-ranching movement whose chief weapon, apart
from meetings, speeches and lobbying of district councils, was cattle driving.
This was at its height in 1907–8 and Ginnell and Sheehy were to the fore. It
involved driving cattle from the graziers' land, generally at night, and leaving
them to wander the roads or putting them into farms some distance away.
Ginnell also referred to this as cattle scattering, 'putting the cattle off a ranch
and scattering them as far and in as many directions as possible.'[15] By November
1907 Judge Curran addressing Trim quarter sessions reported forty cattle
drives in Meath.[16]

The most notable incident in the Dunshaughlin area was in Lagore, near the
town, when sixty-five cattle belonging to local graziers, James Toole of Ratoath,
Thomas Everard of Lagore and John Morrin of Johnstown were driven off and
only twenty-nine discovered the following day despite searches by all the
available police. The previous day thirty-three cattle were driven off Lord
Dunsany's land and 100 more were removed 'a few miles off Dunshaughlin' after
an anti-ranching meeting in the town. The *Meath Herald* reported great unease
'owing to the number of drives and the ease with which they are effected'.[17]

The aim was to deter graziers from renting grassland so efforts were also
made to prevent auctions. When the land at Lagore came up for auction a
fortnight after the cattle drive a meeting arranged to disrupt it was banned by
the police. Seventy-five extra police were brought in by train to prevent the
meeting and in all 140 men were deployed. David Sheehy M.P. and Bernard
Carolan, Secretary of the South Meath branch of the United Irish League,
were stopped at Bonestown near the lands and refused entry. Finally, to avoid
batons being used on the crowd Sheehy agreed to hold the meeting in Ratoath.
The auction went ahead with the auctioneer reporting he had sold all 400
acres at prices from £2 to £4 an acre, all those who previously held the land
taking it again.[18] By May 1908 twenty-six farms totalling 3,208 acres were
unlet in the county.[19] However, it seems that many farms were let in the
parish and surrounding areas in this period and organized opposition to it
seems to have been limited and ineffective. A year later only 561 acres were
unlet in the whole county according to police reports.[20]

As part of his campaign to subdivide the rich grasslands Ginnell was
successful in having the government compile a list of all the untenanted land
in the country.[21] Untenanted land was defined as land in which the owner in
fee had created no tenancy, so it was farmed by the owner in fee or let

temporarily, generally for eleven months. It was not necessarily unoccupied land.[22] The return published in 1908 showed that thousands of acres in each county were untenanted, many without even a herd's house. The issue was regularly highlighted in parliament, at meetings throughout Meath which were extensively reported in the local press and Ginnell also addressed a number of district councils, including Dunshaughlin, on the issue. Ginnell was eventually imprisoned for six months for contempt of court and availed of the time to write *Land and Liberty*, a denunciation of ranching, grazing and the eleven month system.

Nevertheless, as demonstrated in the previous chapter there was in fact very little change in Dunshaughlin in the ownership of the substantial farms prior to World War I and there was little or no subdivision despite the agitation and cattle drives. There are, it appears, a number of reasons for this. Although local and national activists spoke of great swathes of land suitable for sub-division only a small minority of owners would sell without an element of compulsion and the land acts did not give the Estates Commissioners such power. Vigilance Committees were established in a number of areas in Meath to campaign for the purchase of local estates by the Estates Commissioners for redistribution among those with uneconomic holdings, farmers' sons and labourers. A Dunshaughlin Vigilance Committee was formed in 1909 but found few landlords in the vicinity willing to sell. The owner of Lagore, Lord Trimlestown, wrote 'I wish to state that I have no present intentions of selling my property at Big Lagore to the Estates Commissioners.'[23] Four months later it was up for *public* auction. The Committee seems to have lapsed and in 1914 the District Council chairman, P.J. Mulvany, acknowledged that without a change in the land acts 'we had no means at our disposal to compel them so consequently we had to rest on our oars.'[24]

The return of untenanted land recorded almost 3,500 acres in the parish in this category and by implication suitable for subdivision.[25] An analysis of the individual estates or farms listed suggests however that a number of them were unlikely candidates for division, being held by long standing owners. In Woodtown Edward Delany's eldest son William held 112 acres and though he now lived in Colgath, near Kilcock, almost ten miles away, this land had been farmed by the Delanys for almost a century. Another 100 acres of Delany land in Bedfanstown was held by William's cousin, also William, who lived in Navan and this land had been in the family since the 1850s at least. Neither was likely to accept voluntary subdivision. A ninety-five acre farm in Derrockstown which was also listed belonged to Angelo Murphy. Both the 1901 and 1911 census record him as resident on the land which Thomas and John Murphy bought in 1862.[26] Lord Dunsany held almost 200 acres which he was unlikely to sell as it was within half a mile of Dunsany Castle.

The largest owners of untenanted land were Mrs. Annette and Tom Leonard with over 1,000 acres in Knockmark and Warrenstown, James McCann who had

660 acres in Culmullen, John Leonard with over 500 acres in Culmullen, Curraghtown and Pelletstown, Patrick Donegan in possession of 227 acres in Derrockstown and Lady Mowbray and Stourton holding 200 acres in Curraghtown and Hayestown.

Mrs. Leonard's property consisted of two large holdings, 656 acres in Warrenstown and 487 in Knockmark with only two tenants on the former, a mason and a shepherd, and a herd's house on the latter. Annette Leonard's family, the Johnstons, had held land here for over 200 years and her husband Tom farmed extensively up to 1900 at least.[27] At the inaugural meeting of the Warrenstown branch of the United Irish League in 1914 a member of the district council, Michael Fitzimons from Dunsany, urged members to 'use their power to compel the ranch holders, the graziers and the land sharks to give up the land for division among the people' and he looked forward to the day when 'those large green fields around us will become the homes of a prosperous and contented people'.[28] However, the Warrenstown farm was not subdivided and following Tom Leonard's death in 1920 it eventually became the property of the Salesian Fathers who run it to the present day as an agricultural college.[29]

The lands owned by James McCann seemed to present a better prospect for division. They had been sold on two occasions during the nineteenth century under the Incumbered Estates Acts. It has not been possible to trace when the McCanns came into ownership but it seems certain the lands were regularly let for grazing. James McCann was an M.P. who lived in Donnybrook and held over 1000 acres in Meath in 1876.[30] The *Meath Chronicle* claimed that he devoted much of his vast fortune to reviving native industry and repeopling the land while Dunshaughlin rural district council passed a motion of sympathy on his death saying he had done much to stem the tide of emigration by breaking up the grazing ranches.[31] There is little evidence for this in Dunshaughlin for the family retained all the land until 1917 when John Leonard bought it from them, selling his property in Pelletstown at the same time. John Leonard, who until then had lived in Dublin and Macetown, Skryne took up residence in Culmullen in 1917–18.[32] Most of the remaining tracts of untenanted land survived intact beyond the period covered in this book. Lady Mowbray and Stourton was a daughter of Matthew E. Corbally, of Corbalton Hall near Dunshaughlin; he had been M.P. for Meath in 1840–1 and 1842–71. The Corbally family had owned land in Hayestown and Curraghtown since at least 1854 as well as land in Creemore in the adjoining parish of Batterstown.[33] The Culmullen Vigilance Committee was hopeful that the Estates Commissioners would purchase some of the lands, describing her ladyship as 'a good charitable lady' whose people had not cleared out families in 'penal times'.[34] However no progress in this direction was made in Hayestown until the 1920s but about seventy-five acres in Curraghtown were transferred to the occupants before 1914. Donegan's land in Derrockstown was eventually divided in the 1950s when a number of families from Mayo availed of the Land Commission's policy of providing economic holdings in Meath for farmers living on congested non-viable farms in the west.[35]

Thus, efforts prior to 1914 to divide large farms in the parish were singularly unsuccessful and most of those listed as untenanted in 1908 remained intact for many years. Neither rhetoric nor short lived cattle driving had an appreciable effect in the absence of compulsory purchase powers. Nevertheless, in parts of Meath like Oldcastle in the north where stronger opposition had been mounted some lands had been divided.[36] Agitation in Dunshaughlin had little effect, for apart from the lack of compulsory purchase and the long standing status of most owners opposition was neither concerted nor continuous. The United Irish League had a fitful existence in the parish, affiliation to the national body being paid irregularly.[37] P.J. Mulvany was president, and Bernard Carolan secretary, of the South Meath executive for a number of years but Carolan was forced to resign in 1908 after supporting the readmission of William O Brien and Tim Healy to the Irish Party.[38] Mulvany also dropped out and it seems Dunshaughlin was only rarely represented at meetings afterwards. While in office Carolan had expressed reservations about cattle driving, suggesting it be done by day, while Mulvany said night driving gave an opportunity to land grabbers to turn out their cattle and get damages in the courts.[39]

These reservations about cattle driving reflected similar doubts at national level and John Redmond rarely gave the tactic more than lukewarm support.[40] The reality was that this phase of the land struggle was much more complex than the Land League era when nationalists could present the struggle in black and white terms of the rack-rented native tenant against the foreign grasping landlord. Now it was more often Irishman against Irishman and neighbour against neighbour, for many of the most influential members of the United Irish League nationally and locally, were themselves landowners. Ginnell had to admit that some of the eleven month men 'are excellent Nationalists'[41] and in Dunshaughlin people like Mulvany and Delany held substantial farms. In such circumstances there were bound to be reservations about the wisdom of Ginnell's campaign. When he addressed the Dunshaughlin council in 1907 there was opposition to him addressing the meeting. Mrs. Leonard stated, 'I am afraid that the graziers will have to leave the room' and eventually half of those present, including Mrs. Leonard, left on the pretext of going to a funeral. However Mulvany stayed to chair the meeting.[42] A more Nationalist council was elected in 1908, Mrs. Leonard polled lowest of three candidates in her division and a later attempt to have her co-opted failed.[43]

Other organizations also failed to make any impact in Dunshaughlin. Carolan became Secretary of a Land and Labour Association in 1906 but it seems to have lapsed almost immediately[44] while reference has already been made to the brief flowering of the Vigilance Committee. Throughout the decade the Meath Labour Union prospered in the county but no branch was formed in Dunshaughlin despite the efforts of neighbouring branches. In summary, while some attempts were made, opposition to the status quo was sporadic and ineffective.

The previous chapter has referred to the condition of the agricultural labourers in the nineteenth century and to some improvement in their conditions, particularly housing. Progress in this area was maintained in the first decade of the new century.

Following the Local Government Act of 1898 the newly formed rural district councils were given responsibility for the implementation of the Labourers' Acts. As the councillors were locally elected they tended to support labourers' applications for cottages but the expenditure involved had implications for the rates, as loans received from the Local Government Board had to be repaid. Thus, councils had to strike a balance between responding to the labourers' demands for housing and the farmers' opposition to higher rates. In Dunshaughlin in 1906 the levy was 2¼d. in the pound, thus a council member like P.J. Mulvany who had land rated at £140 paid £1.6s. 3d. per annum towards the provision of cottages. The labourer in receipt of the house paid an average of 1s. 3d. rent weekly, amounting to £3.5s. per year.[45]

A new Labourers' Act became law in 1906 and the following year the Local Government Board issued a set of sample plans to the councils. It proposed that, as five was the average number in an agricultural labourer's family, four rooms were required, a living room or kitchen and three bedrooms. Great emphasis was placed on the choice of a dry site and effective ventilation with a fire place per room due to the prevalence of tuberculosis, bronchitis and other respiratory diseases. Councils were asked not to exceed £130 in building the houses.[46]

As part of the procedure for erecting a cottage local public inquiries were held into labourers' applications. Bernard Carolan advised the labourers to look after their own interests, claiming the Dunshaughlin council would exclude the press so 'ranchers and would-be ranchers' could discuss the best way 'the labourer can be cheated'. Prior to the hearing he arranged a solicitor to represent applicants at the inquiry at a shilling each.[47] Carolan however had a vested interest in the cottages for he was given a number of the building contracts by the council. Contrary to his warnings the hearings were open and the proceedings provide an insight into attitudes and housing conditions in the area.

A number of land owners such as Patrick Donegan in Derrockstown and Thomas Delany in Roestown had no objection to granting sites. Mrs. Annette Leonard agreed to two on her lands and her husband Tom was described by a local councillor as 'a most excellent landlord.' Patrick Murphy opposed a cottage in Cooksland as he had already granted one site and there were three other houses on the property occupied by a mason, a carpenter and a policeman. Thomas B. Donnelly, a J.P. who lived in Knockmark with seven servants, held sixty acres in Leshemstown and had dubious grounds for objecting, claiming he used the holding as a stud farm, but said he would erect a cottage at his own expense and give half an acre with it if the Inspector considered a cottage necessary. The medical officer for the council reported that the applicant's house was in a wretched condition and unfit for human habitation. Thomas Anderson, a labourer applying for a cottage in Roestown stated that rain came through the roof of his home and 'it gives me enough to do to carry my feet to bed at night on account of sticking so firm in the mud that forms the floor.' The landowner Mr. Val McDermott eventually consented to an alternative site to the one requested. Anderson was not working for McDermott but feared if he applied for a cottage on his employer's land, a Mrs. Dyas, he would be dismissed.

Though a number of homes were declared unfit for habitation, conditions in general appear to have been worse in other parts of the district where applicants described living in 'a lump of mud', 'the side of a ditch' and in a one roomed dwelling housing ten people.[48] Twenty-three of the ninety-six applications were rejected, as in the country as a whole 47,000 applications were made for an available 25,000 cottages and the inspector sanctioned 'only those in which necessity was proven beyond doubt.'[49]

The cost of building rarely remained at the recommended £130, ranging from £137 to £145 in 1908 in easily accessible sites. In a number of cases the council found it difficult to get contractors, especially in outlying areas. Carolan tendered at £155 for cottages in Baltrasna and Woodtown and Edward Delany agreed with him that it was not possible to build houses in such areas within £20 of the cost of a house near the town.[50] On average the council paid £40 to the farmers for the plots.[51]

There was a very favourable reaction to the cottages. The national directory of the United Irish League said that the Labourers' Acts 'yielded most satisfactory results' and labourers had changed their 'former miserable dwellings for decent, roomy, sanitary houses,' while in 1912 it claimed 'there is nothing to equal the provision for agricultural labourers in any country in Europe or out of it.'[52]

The 1911 census report acknowledged that many labourers were now accommodated in second class homes, 'a class originally intended mainly for dwellings of the character of good farm houses.'[53] The improvement in Dunshaughlin parish is reflected in the fact that 73 per cent of houses where the head was an agricultural or farm labourer, herd or shepherd were second class houses with 26 per cent in third class. In 1901 just below half were in second class houses.[54]

The 1911 report on the wages of agricultural labourers claims that cash wages 'have increased continuously for many years past' but that real wages had improved little due to a fall in the value of money. The 1911 figures for general labourers in Meath range from 10s. 6d. to 12s. per week.[55] In the Dunshaughlin area however, wages do not seem to have improved much between 1901 and 1911. In a court case in 1906 John McEntee, a Derrockstown farmer, was sued for wages due to Patrick Connor who had been hired at 7*s*. per week plus meals. Thomas Dowd had 10*s*. weekly from one of the substantial landholders, Edward Kelly, but complained that his wages were cut every wet day.[56] In 1914 at a joint meeting of the Meath Labour Union and the Farmers' Association it was agreed that 12*s*. weekly should be the norm for a labourer in constant employment as wages of 10*s*. and even 9*s*. were common.[57] Such low wages eventually led to conflict in the Dunshaughlin area in 1919 which involved strikes by agricultural labourers and picketing of railway stations to deny the farmers access to the Dublin cattle market.[58]

Another source of employment for the farm worker was road work. Traditionally such work had been done on contract, often taken by farmers during the winter, but following pressure by the Meath Labour Union the county council agreed to a scheme of direct labour whereby labourers would be employed by the council. In 1907 the rates of pay were 2*s*. per day and 13*s*. a week after a year's satisfactory service.[59]

Thus, while housing conditions undoubtedly improved for many farm labourers, wages were still very low and unless a man was in regular employment work could be seasonal, irregular and dependent on the weather. Most of the population appear to have bought food and clothing on credit, paying off small sums irregularly. Accounts from Peadar Murray's general purpose store and public house in Dunshaughlin survive for 1900 and contain details of purchases and payments from all sections of the community. Patrick Hand of Derrockstown was a shepherd with three sons ranging in age from fifteen to twenty-six – each an agricultural labourer – a wife and a daughter. He had no land. From August to November 1900 he owed amounts varying from £2. 8*s*. 6*d*. to £4. 16*s*. 7*d*., paying off £1. 7*s*. and 1*s*. 10*d*. on 12 and 17 September respectively and £1. 5*s*. 11*d*. on 1 October. His purchases included tea and sugar, wheaten flour, meal, drapery, boots and various goods not itemized. James Lynch, an unmarried labourer from Redbog owed from 15*s*. to £2. 6*s*. 6*d*. and paid off 15*s*. and 14*s*. 6*d*. on 26 September and 15 November. Most of his purchases are returned as 'goods' but butter, stout and tobacco are mentioned. Michael Bracken, who had five acres in Red Bog but returned himself as a farmer in 1901, made payments in cash and in kind to Murrays, the latter consisting of butter and eggs.[60] Clearly for many people survival depended on the availability of credit in the local store.

The community revealed in this study is one that was polarized socially and economically. The substantial farmers and even the medium farmers were numerically small but controlled most of the land of the parish, they tended to retain and consolidate their property and were influential in local politics. The rural labourers experienced some improvement in housing but low wages and lack of regular employment were issues which would lead to conflict in the future.

Conclusion

This study has examined developments in a small rural community from 1854 to 1914, from the aftermath of the Famine to the approach of the first world war. It has focused on three groups, the large or substantial farmer with 100 acres or more, the medium sized farmer with less than 100 acres and the landless or almost landless agricultural labourer. A number of aspects were analysed such as the distribution of farms of various sizes and the extent of change in the distribution over sixty years, and the degree of permanence or displacement of farming families in the area during this time span.

Central to an understanding of the period is the unrelenting decline in tillage from mid-century and the corresponding expansion of grassland and cattle fattening. This was a national trend but it was most pronounced in eastern counties, and the poor law union of Dunshaughlin outscored every other union in the country in the proportion of its area under grass. Few other areas came close to matching it in this respect.

Changes in the use of land have implications for the social structure of an area and this is particularly true in the case of the transfer from tillage to pasture. Cattle fattening had a low labour requirement, particularly when based on summer grazing. The grazier's family, with the assistance of a herd or shepherd and some casual labour when required, was sufficient to maintain the farm. Thus, the agricultural labourer found it increasingly difficult to get work and there was a precipitous decline in numbers among this class from 1854 to 1914. If it were not for the provision of labourers' cottages by the rural council from the 1890s the decline would probably be even more pronounced.

On the other hand the graziers, their farms and homes were a more permanent feature of the landscape. Of the forty-five farms of 100 acres and above in the parish in 1854, thirty-nine were still in existence sixty years later. Families who dominated this sector in 1854 such as the Delanys, Leonards, Kelly, Mulvany, Geraghty, Murphy and Daly retained and often extended their holdings over the six decades. Although many held their land on lease they were the dominant social class in the area as the head landlords or landowners such as Hans H. Woods, Thomas E. Taylor and the Supples were practically all absentees. A number benefited from substantial profits, especially from 1850–70 and some like Edward Delany were able to purchase land they previously held on long leases. These farmers tended to intermarry and to dominate local government, until 1908 at least. Though Catholic and moderate

57

nationalists like the majority of the population their wealth and status set them apart from their co-parishioners.

The early twentieth century landscape was often one of whole townlands with a handful of houses and fields given over to grass. The anti-grazing movement however never developed as a powerful force in Dunshaughlin. This was partly because most of the graziers were long standing members of the community, unlike those in other parts of the country who were seen to have taken land rightfully belonging to evicted tenants, and partly because opposition was sporadic and poorly organised. Laurence Ginnell, the chief anti-grazing activist in Leinster, speaking to Dunshaughlin rural district council in 1907, urged local smallholders and farmers' sons to be much more active in demanding land. If they did not the Estates Commissioners would, he prophesied, buy up local untenanted land 'and there will be people brought in from Counties Mayo or Donegal or some western county and planted there in County Meath, and the Meath men will wonder then how it was that the strangers came in and got the land at their doors while themselves were asleep.'[1] Ginnell was, in fact, more far seeing than probably even he realised for migration from western congested areas would become government policy in the 1930s and it would lead to radical change in population and landscape in a number of townlands.

Appendices

TOWNLANDS OF DUNSHAUGHLIN ROMAN CATHOLIC PARISH

Culmullen	*Dunshaughlin*	*Knockmark*
Baltrasna	Ballinlough	Augherskea
Ballynare	Ballymurphy	Baronstown
Barstown	Bonestown	Bedfanstown
Bogganstown	Clonross	Drumree
Cullendragh	Cooksland	Glane Great
Culcommon	Derrockstown	Glane Little
Culmullen	Dunshaughlin	Kilcooley
Cultromer	Gaulstown	Knockmark
Curraghtown	Grangend	Merrywell
Gaulstown	Grangend Common	Mooretown
Hayestown	Johnstown	Warrenstown
Warrenstown	Knocks	
Woodcockstown	Leshemstown	
Woodtown	Merrywell	
	Pelletstown	
	Rathhill	
	Readsland	
	Redbog	
	Roestown	
	Thomastown	

APPENDIX 2

POPULATION AND HOUSE NUMBERS BY TOWNLAND, 1841–51

Dunshaughlin Civil Parish

| | 1841 | | 1851 | | Percentage |
	Houses	Population	Houses	Population	Pop. Change
Ballinlough	2	49	3	6	See note
Ballymurphy	3	15	3	13	−13
Bonestown	1	10	4	13	+30
Clonross	2	16	4	37	+131
Cooksland	20	115	9	44	−62
Derrockstown	6	40	8	36	−10
Dunshaughlin	38	169	24	87	−49
Gaulstown	2	17	2	18	+6
Grangend	14	59	11	35	−41
Johnstown	6	26	4	20	−23
Knocks	0	0	1	4	N/A
Leshemstown	13	51	9	40	−22
Merrywell	7	45	3	15	−67
Pelletstown	25	125	21	103	−18
Rathhill	3	18	3	25	+39
Readsland	10	52	12	40	−23
Redbog	26	145	32	132	−9
Roestown	15	95	15	71	−25
Thomastown	2	10	1	6	−40
Rural total	**195**	**1057**	**169**	**745**	**−30**
Dunsh'lin Town	100	524	93	422	−19

Note: The 1841 figures for Ballinlough probably includes builders of the Workhouse which wasn't opened until May 1841.

Culmullen Civil Parish

| | 1841 | | 1851 | | Percentage |
	Houses	*Population*	*Houses*	*Population*	*Pop. Change*
Baltrasna	15	81	14	65	−20
Ballynare	1	5	2	12	+140
Barstown	9	50	9	50	0
Bogganstown	18	111	14	62	−44
Cullendragh	9	43	8	42	−2
Culmullen	17	91	12	50	−45
Cultromer	15	90	17	101	+12
Curraghtown	36	182	30	153	−16
Gaulstown	10	78	7	57	−27
Hayestown	1	9	1	5	−44
Warrenstown	6	24	5	22	−8
Woodcockstown	20	89	11	49	−45
Woodtown	21	137	12	85	−38
Culcommon	2	20	0	0	−100
Parish total	**180**	**1010**	**142**	**735**	**−27**

Note: Culcommon townland is in the civil parish of Culmullen but is in the barony of Upper Deece.

Knockmark Civil Parish

| | 1841 | | 1851 | | Percentage |
	Houses	*Population*	*Houses*	*Population*	*Pop. Change*
Augherskea	50	278	40	204	−27
Baronstown	0	0	1	6	N/A
Bedfanstown	4	15	4	10	−33
Drumree	7	27	2	10	−63
Glane Great	1	5	6	32	+540
Glane Litle	2	14	2	10	−29
Kilcooley	2	19	2	15	−21
Knockmark	29	147	29	127	−14
Merrywell	6	23	6	28	−22
Moorestown	3	25	1	9	−64
Warrenstown	13	77	1	76	−1
Parish Total	**117**	**630**	**104**	**527**	**−16**

APPENDIX 3

FARMERS WITH OVER 100 ACRES 1854 AND *c*.1911

Townland	1854 *Occupier*	*Area* a.r.p.	*c*.1911 *Occupier*	*Area* a.r.p.
Ballinlough	James Mulvany	198:0:29	Patrick Mulvany	197:0:19
Ballymurphy	Richard Barnewall	172:2:36	John Morrin	172:1:29
Bonestown	James Kelly	288:0:34	Edward Kelly	287:1:31
Clonross	John Daly	171:2:29	Isabella Daly	172:3:28
Cooksland	William Murphy	129:2:33	Reps. Patk. Murphy	127:2:03
Derrockstown	Edward Delany	251:1:04	Patrick Donegan	227:3:36
Derrockstown	Eliz. McDonnell	103:0:21	Angelo Murphy	95:2:01
Dunshaughlin	David W. Supple	128:3:04	Angelo Murphy	128:3:08
Gaulstown	Robert Morris	115:3:39	Rosanna Morris	116:3:02
Johnstown	Thomas Murphy	195:3:21	John Murphy	195:3:21
Johnstown	John Morrin	222:2:25	John Morrin	220:2:25
Leshemstown	Willoughby Bond	329:3:21	Val. McDermott	329:3:21
Merrywell	Thomas Gerarty	121:3:33	Hugh Gearty	121:3:33
Pelletstown	John Johnson	162:0:09	John Leonard	163:0:02
Rath Hill	Patrick Mullen	134:0:08	Reps.Ptk. Murphy	134:0:08
Readsland	John Ball	107:0:33	George Ball	107:0:33
Roestown	James Maher	167:1:27	Val. McDermott	167:1:27
Thomastown	James Kelly	187:3:19	Edward Kelly	187:3:19
Barstown	Edward Gallagher	188:0:06	Michael Kiernan	95:0:26
			Reps. J. Collins	92:2:18
Cullendragh	William Gray	232:0:28	Henry Black	233:3:18
Culcommon	Philip Grierson	156:1:27	Richard Nash	166:2:03
Culmullen	Nicholas Sadleir	184:1:18	John Leonard	85:1:35
			John Leonard	98:2:13
Culmullen	Matthew Beggs	190:1:38	Arthur McCann	190:1:38
Culmullen	William Coffey	343:1:03	Patrick Mulloy	342:3:03
Culmullen	James Kearney	187:1:23	Arthur McCann	187:1:23
Culmullen	Patrick Leonard	147:3:05	John Leonard	147:3:05
			John Leonard	85:0:24
			John Leonard	24:2:35
Cultromer	John Daly	221:1:19	Gerald Daly	221:1:19
Curraghtown	Matthew Ennis	125:3:06	Reps. A. Roche	125:3:06
Curraghtown	Dowdall & Byrne	124:3:18	Michael Byrne	130:0:01
Gaulstown	James Barrington	106:3:35	John Barrington	106:3:35
Gaulstown	Michael Lawless	108:0:10	Michael McKenna	107:3:10
Gaulstown	Michael Lawless	116:0:37	Michael McKenna	116:0:37
Hayestown	Matthew Corbally	124:1:39	Lady Mowbray &c.	124:1:39
Warrenstown	Patrick McGerr	167:0:17	Patrick Leonard	168:2:35
Woodcockstown	Edward Gallagher	100:2:01	Patrick Mulloy	99:1:31
Woodtown	Bridget Delany	112:2:21	William Delany	112:2:21
Woodtown	Philip Purdon	198:2:23	Patrick Flanagan	198:2:23

Appendix 3 contd.

Townland	Occupier	Area a.r.p.	Occupier	Area a.r.p.
Woodtown	John P. Brett	209:0:39	Edward Delany	209:0:39
Woodtown	Edward Delany	179:3:39	Edward Delany	178:3:39
Bedfanstown	Edward Delany	104:1:24	William Delany	103:1:14
Glane Gt.	Rev. J. Burnett	110:3:29	Lord Dunsany	114:2:04
Knockmark	Eliza Johnson	499:0:00	Mrs. A. Leonard	487:1:12
Mooretown	Patrick Keena	258:3:08	Thomas Leonard	258:1:14
Warrenstown	Eliza Johnson	673:0:21	Mrs. A. Leonard	656:0:04

APPENDIX 4

STOCKING RATES PER 100 ACRES, DUNSHAUGHLIN P.L.U. 1851–1911

	No of Livestock Units	Area of Grassland & Meadow	Livestock Units per 100 acres
1851	28250	78543	36.0
1856	34928	83407(e)	41.9
1861	38217	88251(e)	43.3
1866	36924	90769(e)	40.7
1871	41087	92675(e)	44.3
1876	42579	96779	44.0
1881	40710	96965	42.0
1886	44554	97855	45.5
1891	44340	98643	45.0
1896	49598	99192	50.0
1901	52628	98508	53.4
1906	49541	98554	50.3
1911	50805	97377	52.2

Note: Figures based on agricultural statistics for the years concerned. Livestock units were calculated according to the scheme used in Department of Agriculture and Food, *CAP reform: Livestock, cattle and sheep schemes* (Dublin, 1993), p. 17, supplemented by Jones, *Graziers, land reform and political conflict*, p. 57. Accordingly, cows, cattle and horses of 2 years and above were rated as 1 livestock unit (L.U.), cattle and horses of 1 to 2 years were 0.6 L.Us, those less than 1 year were equivalent to 0.3 L.Us, asses and mules were 0.5 L.Us and sheep were 0.15 L.Us.

Area figures followed by (e) indicate that it was necessary to estimate the acreage given over to grassland. This was done by subtracting the total acreage for crops, including meadow, woods, bogs, water, roads etc. from the total area of the Union.

APPENDIX 5

FARM ACCOUNTS SUMMARY: EDWARD DELANY

Year	Purchases	Sales	Gross Income	Net Income
1852–53	£1,237	£1,853	£616	£274
1853–54	£1,390	£2,075	£686	£344
1854–55	£1,722	£2,240	£518	£176
1855–56	£1,510	£2,134	£624	£282
1856–57	£1,409	£2,019	£610	£268
1857–58	N/A	N/A	N/A	N/A
1858–59	£1,560	£2,063	£556	£214
1859–60	£1,560	£2,237	£677	£335
1860–61	£1,465	£2,067	£602	£260
1861–62	£1,547	£2,059	£512	£170
1862–63	£1,663	£2,278	£615	£273
1863–64	£1,706	£2,233	£727	£385
1864–65	£1,770	£2,457	£687	£345
1865–66	£1,948	£2,676	£728	£386
1866–67	£2,024	£2,664	£640	£298
1867–68	£1,947	£2,624	£677	£335
1868–69	£1,961	£2,815	£854	£512
1869–70	£2,019	£2,763	£744	£402
1870–71	£2,066	£2,846	£780	£438
1871–72	£2,200	£2,978	£778	£473
1872–73	£2,299	£2,963	£664	£359
1873–74	£2,215	£2,835	£620	£315
1874–75	£2,237	£2,876	£638	£363
1875–76	£2,564	£3,294	£730	£455
1876–77	£2,234	£2,901	£667	£392
1877–78	£2,539	£3,133	£594	£319
1878–79	£2,230	£2,555	£325	£50
1879–80	£1,961	£2,644	£683	£408
1880–81	N/A	N/A	N/A	N/A
1881–82	£2,247	£3,083	£835	£560
1882–83	N/A	N/A	N/A	N/A
1883–84	£2,437	£2,956	£519	£244
1884–85	£2,286	£2,741	£455	£180
1885–86	£1,859	£2,418	£559	£284
1886–87	£1,974	£2,417	£444	£169
1887–88	£1,710	£2,443	£733	£458
1888–89	£2,070	£2,653	£584	£309
1889–90	£3,185	£3,983	£780	£203
1890–91	£3,109	£3,825	£716	£121
1891–92	£2,935	£3,753	£817	£222
1892–93	£2,726	£3,815	£1,089	£494
1893–94	£2,951	£4,022	£1,071	£476
1894–95	£3,013	£4,035	£1,022	£427
1895–96	£3,111	£3,919	£808	£213
1896–97	£2,425	£3,234	£809	£214
1897–98	£2,416	£3,165	£749	£154
1898–99	£2,287	£3,107	£820	£225

Source: Farm account books of Edward Delany, NLI, MSS 19347–8. N/A: Not available

Notes

CSORP	Chief Secretary's Office Registered Papers
DED	District Electoral Division
GO	Genealogical Office
H.C.	House of Commons
LEC	Landed Estates Court
NA	National Archives
NLI	National Library of Ireland
PLG	Poor Law Guardian
RD	Registry of Deeds
TAB	Tithe Applotment Books

In the initial reference to any parliamentary paper the printed pagination is given immediately after the paper's title and the manuscript pagination is given at the end of the footnote. However, in second and subsequent references to a paper a shortened title is used and the printed pagination only is given.

INTRODUCTION

1 *Drogheda Independent*, 12 May 1900.
2 William Bulfin, *Rambles in Eirinn*, (Dublin 1907), p. 89.
3 W.E. Vaughan, 'Farmer, grazier and gentleman: Edward Delany of Woodtown, 1851–99', *Irish Economic and Social History*, ix, (1982), pp 53–72.
4 D.S. Jones, *Graziers, land reform and political conflict in Ireland*, (Washington, 1995).
5 *The parliamentary gazetteer of Ireland, 1844–45*, (2 vols, Dublin, 1845), ii, p. 164.
6 *Report from the select committee appointed to inquire whether the present townland valuation of Ireland made by the committee of valuation under the act 16 Vict. c. 52, can be made available for the imposition of poor rate and other local rates in that country*, pp iii–iv (513), H.C. 1844, vii, 463–4.

7 Jones, *Graziers, land reform and political conflict in Ireland*, p. 97.
8 William Nolan, *Fassadinin*, (Dublin, 1979), p. 153.
9 *Return of the several counties, counties of cities, and counties of towns in Ireland, of which the valuation under the act 9 and 10 Vict. c. 110, has been completed*, p. 11, (553), H.C. 1852, xlvii, 547.
10 *General valuation of rateable property in Ireland, Union of Dunshaughlin, valuation of the several tenements*, (Dublin, 1854), pp 72–74, 56–57, 58–59 and 85–86 respectively. (Cited hereafter as *General valuation . . . Union of Dunshaughlin*.)
11 All calculations based on census of population figures for 1841 and 1851. See *The census of Ireland for the year 1851 showing the area population and number of houses by townlands and electoral divisions, vol. i, county of*

Meath, p. 226 [1494], H.C. 1852, xlvi, 598.

12 Details which follow are taken from General valuation ... *Union of Dunshaughlin*, and figures for land outside the parish refer to 1876 and are from *Returns of the owners of land of one acre and upwards in counties, counties of cities and counties of towns in Ireland*, pp 65–74 [C 1492], H.C. 1876, lxxx, 133–142.

13 L.G. Pine (ed.), *Burke's genealogical and heraldic history of the landed gentry of Ireland* (4th ed., London, 1958), p. 750.

14 R. Keane, A. Hughes, R. Swan (eds.), *Ardgillan Castle and the Taylor family* (Dublin, 1995), pp 31–38.

15 *Thom's directory, 1873* (Dublin, 1873), p. 248.

16 RD, 1862/21/217.

17 NA, Landed Estate Court Rentals, vol. 1, no. 63, 21 June 1850. Cited hereafter as LEC Rentals.

LAND AND AGRICULTURE AFTER
THE FAMINE

1 *Report from the select committee appointed to inquire into the present state of agriculture, and persons employed in agriculture in the United Kingdom, with minutes of evidence, appendix, and index*, p. 497, H.C. 1833 (612), v, no manuscript pagination.

2 *First report of inquiry into the conditions of the poorer classes in Ireland: supplement to appendix E*, p. 112 [37], H.C. 1836, xxxii, 224.

3 Until 1900 the government's annual statistics include meadow and clover as crops but from 1901 they were regarded as grassland 'to distinguish ... land under the plough from land given over to stock rearing, or ... pastoral land', see *Agricultural statistics of Ireland with a detailed report on agriculture, for the year 1901*, p. vi, [Cd 1170], H.C. 1902, cxvi, 325. I have adopted this practice for each year from 1851, total tillage representing total extent under crops minus extent under meadow and clover.

4 *Census of Ireland for the year 1851, pt. ii: returns of agricultural produce in 1851*, p. 242 [1589], H.C. 1852–53, xciii, 280 and *Agricultural statistics of Ireland ... 1901*, p. 25.

5 *Agricultural statistics of Ireland, with a detailed report on agriculture, for the year 1911*, p. vi [Cd 6377], H.C. 1912–13, cvi, 738.

6 *Census of Ireland 1851, pt. ii., returns of agricultural produce, 1851*, pp xi–xii and *Agricultural statistics of Ireland ... 1911*, p. 3, for Meath. Union figures calculated from Table 2.

7 *Census of Ireland 1851, pt. ii: returns of agricultural produce, 1851*, p. 676 and *Agricultural statistics of Ireland for the year 1861*, p. 150 [3156], H.C. 1863, lxix, 764.

8 NA, LEC Rentals, vol. 1, no 63, 21 June 1850.

9 NA, LEC Rentals, vol. 62, no. 54, 6 July 1861.

10 NA, LEC Rentals, vol. 82, no. 26, 3 July 1866.

11 NA, LEC Rentals, vol. 99, no. 31, 11 Nov. 1870.

12 NA, LEC Rentals, vol. 106, no. 2, 3 May 1872.

13 NA, LEC Rentals, vol. 146, no. 25, 14 March 1884.

14 NA, LEC Rentals, vol. 149, no. 61, 6 Nov. 1885.

15 *Drogheda Independent*, 12 May 1900.

16 James Donnelly, jun., 'Landlords and tenants' in W.E. Vaughan (ed.), *A new history of Ireland, v: Ireland under the Union, i* (Oxford, 1989), pp 347–9.

17 *Return of the proceedings of the commissioners for the sale of incumbered estates in Ireland from their commencement up to 1 January 1852 &c.*, p. 5, H.C. 1852 (167), xlvii, 417 and NA, LEC Rentals, vol. 1, no. 63, 21 June 1850.

18 *Dublin Evening Post*, 22 June 1850.
19 *Thom's Directory*, 1851, p. 590.
20 See RD, 1859/23/183 and *Thom's Directory 1872*, p. 1456.
21 NA, LEC Rentals, vol. 54, no. 5, 19 Nov. 1858 and RD, 1859/3/168.
22 *General valuation . . . Union of Dunshaughlin*, p. 78.
23 *Minutes of evidence taken before the departmental committee appointed by the Board of Agriculture to inquire into the inland transit of cattle; with appendices and index*, p. 46 [C 8929], H.C. 1898, xxxiv, 78. (Cited hereafter as *Inland transit committee, minutes of evidence*).
24 RD, 1871/1/9 and 1871/1/10.
25 *Return of owners of land of one acre and upwards*, p. 166.
26 *Dublin Evening Post*, 22 June 1850.
27 RD, 1872/25/167.
28 NA, Land Law Ireland Act 1881, Notices to Fix Fair Rents, 1887–1888, Co. Meath, nos. 430–439, 1C/50/91.
29 RD, 1871/17/132 and 1871/17/133.
30 RD, 1867/22/176 and 1871/41/63.
31 RD, 1862/10/135.
32 NA, Probate Book 1888–92, T 14128, pp 50–52, Murphy, Thomas, Dunshaughlin, plain copy will.
33 RD, 1851/25/202 and *General valuation . . . Union of Dunshaughlin*, p. 35.
34 *General valuation . . . Union of Dunshaughlin*, p. 58 and *Dublin Evening Post*, 22 June 1850.

THE GRAZIERS' WORLD,
1854–1904

1 See Jones, *Graziers, land reform and political conflict* and Vaughan, 'Farmer, grazier and gentleman', pp 53–72.
2 Bulfin, *Rambles in Eirinn*, (Dublin, 1907), p. 91.
3 M.J. Bonn, *Modern Ireland and her agrarian problem*, translated by T.W. Rolleston, (Dublin, 1906), p. 41.

4 Jones, *Graziers, land reform and political conflict*, p. 7.
5 *Drogheda Independent*, 17 March 1906.
6 Valuation Office, Revised valuation books, no. 1, Culmullen ED.
7 NA, Census of Ireland 1901, Enumerators' Forms, DED 10, Culmullen 1–13 and 27, DED 14, Killeen 1–11 and DED 19, Dunshaughlin Meath, 1–21c.
8 See *Drogheda Independent*, 13 December 1890, 16 February 1907, 2 and 28 November 1907.
9 *Royal commission on labour: assistant commissioners' reports on the agricultural labourer, pt. iv: reports by Mr. Arthur Wilson-Fox*, p. 25 [C 6894–xxi], H.C. 1893–94, xxxvii, 363. (Cited hereafter as *Royal commission on labour, pt. iv*.)
10 NA, Census of Ireland 1901, Meath, DED 10, Culmullen.
11 NA, Tithe Applotment Books, County Meath, Parish of Culmullen, 1827, TAB 22/137.
12 NLI, MSS 19347–8, Farm account-books of Edward Delany, 2 vols, 1852–79, (cited hereafter as Farm acc. Edward Delany, vol. 1 or 2).
13 RD, 1874/34/51.
14 RD, 1871/17/132.
15 RD, 1874/34/52.
16 RD, 1851/16/168.
17 RD, 1878/5/274.
18 NA, LEC Rentals, vol. 84, no. 73, 19 March 1867.
19 Farm acc. Edward Delany, vol. 1 and 2.
20 Farm acc. Edward Delany, vol. 1.
21 Farm acc. Edward Delany, vol. 2.
22 Padraic Colum, *The collected poems of Padraic Colum* (Greenwich, Conn., 1953), p. 84.
23 Tom Harris, 'The fairs and markets of Meath in the nineteenth century', (unpublished M.A. thesis, St. Patrick's College, Maynooth, 1996), p. 35.
24 John O Meara, 'The Meath road,' *Journal of the Irish Railway Record Society*, iv no. 20, (Spring 1957), pp 218–240.

25 Bulfin, *Rambles*, p. 83.
26 *Inland transit committee, minutes of evidence*, p. 120.
27 *Report of the departmental committee appointed by the Board of Agriculture to enquire and report upon the inland transit of cattle* [C 8928], H.C. 1898, xxxiv, 1.
28 *Inland transit committee, minutes of evidence*, p. 88.
29 *Inland transit committee, minutes of evidence*, p. 44.
30 *Inland transit committee, minutes of evidence*, p. 48.
31 Full details of purchases, sales, gross and net income as calculated from the farm accounts are given in Appendix 5. Those differ slightly from Vaughan's figures in Vaughan, 'Farmer Grazier and Gentleman' pp 60–61. Vaughan gives all figures calculated on a base of 100 for 1852 but I have retained the monetary values. I have followed Vaughan in assuming an annual rental of £342, (25% above the tenement valuation) but from 1871 used £305 and from 1874, £275 based on information in leases from those years.
32 Farm acc. Edward Delany, vol. 1.
33 Vaughan, 'Farmer, grazier and gentleman,' p. 64.
34 Farm acc. Edward Delany, vol. 2.
35 *Dublin Evening Post*, 22 June 1850.
36 RD, 1871/17/132.
37 Farm acc. Edward Delany, vol. 1.
38 RD, 1874/34/52.
39 RD, 1897/6/296.
40 Valuation Office, Revised valuation books, no. 1, Culmullen ED.
41 Bulfin, *Rambles*, p. 89.
42 NA, Census 1901, Meath DED 10, Culmullen, no. 13, and NA, Wills and Administrations, 1901.
43 RD, 1901/49/155.
44 RD, 1897/6/296.
45 Calculated from Valuation Office, Revised valuation books, no. 1, Culmullen ED, no. 4, Dunshaughlin ED. and no. 1, Killeen ED.
46 NA, Census of Ireland 1901, Enumerators' forms.
47 NA, Census of Ireland 1911, Enumerators' forms, Meath, DED 14, Killeen, no. 11 and *Drogheda Independent*, 23 May 1908 for evidence of the motor-car.
48 NA, Probate book 1888–1892, T14128, Murphy, Thomas, Dunshaughlin, pp 50–52.
49 RD, 1872/6/248.
50 RD, 1873/32/266.
51 RD, 1873/34/197.
52 Details compiled from : Delany of Woodtown, genealogical details, typescript in possession of Mr. Michael Delany, Gaulstown, Dunshaughlin; GO, MS 182A, pp 79–84, NLI, microfilm P. 8310, *Burke's Irish family records* (1964), pp 304–6, and *General valuation . . . Union of Dunshaughlin*, p. 39.
53 Based on reports of elections and meetings of the P.L.G. board in *Drogheda Independent* and *Meath Herald*.
54 *Drogheda Independent*, 1 April 1893.
55 *Inland transit committee, minutes of evidence*, p. 46.
56 Chronology based on GO, MS 182A, pp 79–84 and typescript family history of the Leonards in possession of Mr. Mickey Kenny, Roestown, Dunshaughlin.
57 *Inland transit committee, minutes of evidence*, p. 87.
58 Based on the advertising columns of the *Drogheda Independent*, 1890–1910.

AGRICULTURAL LABOURERS AND
FARMERS, 1854–1904

1 It should be noted that this does not mean that each of those holdings had separate owners or tenants as many people held more than one holding.

2 All the above calculations are based on *General valuation . . . Union of Dunshaughlin* and General Valuation Office Revised valuation books, no. 1, Culmullen ED, no. 4, Dunshaughlin ED, and no. 1, Killeen ED to 1911.

3 Ibid.

4 RD, 1873/12/73 and 1873/12/65.

5 Portion of Register of Dunshaughlin Girls' National School, 1862–1884, in the possession of Mr. Charles Gallagher, Principal, Dunshaughlin National School and Register of Culmullen Boys' National School, 1894–1991 in the possession of Mrs. Kathleen Noone, Principal, Culmullen National School.

6 See *Drogheda Independent*, 30 Jan. 1909, 10 July 1909.

7 NA, LEC Rentals, vol. 87, no. 39, 19 Nov. 1867 and vol. 90, no. 31, 30 June 1868.

8 NA, LEC Rentals, vol. 106, no. 2, 3 May 1872.

9 NA, LEC Rentals, vol. 1, no. 63, 21 June 1850.

10 NA, LEC Rentals, vol. 99, no. 31, 11 Nov. 1870 and RD, 1874/34/51–2, 1874/33/143–5.

11 *Dublin Evening Post*, 22 June 1850.

12 NA, CSORP 1880/34610, Boycotting placard at Dunshaughlin, (register only), NA, CSORP 1881/36192, Boycotting return, October 1881.

13 See NA, Records of Circuit Court, Co. Meath, Land Law (Ireland) Act 1881, Notices to fix fair rents, 1882–1885, (nos 1–220), 1887–1888 (nos 224–496), 1888 (nos 497–759), 1888–1890 (nos 760–966), 1C/50/90–93 respectively; Originating notices on fair rents 1882–1897, 1C/50/97; Co. Meath Clerk of the Peace, Land Law Ireland Acts 1881 and 1887, Minutes of proceedings books, May 1882–Feb. 1890 and County Court, Minutes of proceedings and orders,

Jan. 1886–Nov. 1887, both 1C/50/66. All the above are held by the National Archives in the Four Courts, Dublin.

14 *Report from the select committee on land acts (Ireland), together with the proceedings of the committee, minutes of evidence, appendices and index*, pp 524, 527, H.C. 1894 (310), xiii, 586, 589.

15 For details see Notices to fix fair rents, nos. 431 (Quinn), 483 (Madden) and 445 (Dowdall); Minutes of proceedings and orders, Jan. 1886–Nov. 1887, record 431 (Quinn), record 433 (Dowdall); Minutes of orders and proceedings books, May 1882–Feb. 1890, no. 445 (Dowdall) and Originating notices to fix fair rents, 1882–1897 for Kevlin, not numbered.

16 Laurence Geary, *The plan of campaign, 1886–1891*, (Cork, 1986), pp 6–7.

17 Based on *General valuation . . . Union of Dunshaughlin*, General Valuation Office, *Revised valuation books* and NA, Census of Ireland 1901, Enumerators' forms, Co. Meath, DEDs 10, 14 and 19. As the rateable valuation includes the value of outoffices as well as the house, a higher valuation doesn't necessarily imply that the house is a higher class than one with a lower value.

18 *General valuation . . . Union of Dunshaughlin*, p. 7.

19 Ibid., pp 10, 50.

20 *Drogheda Argus*, 29 Jan. 1859.

21 *General valuation . . . Union of Dunshaughlin*, p. 50.

22 Ibid., pp 9, 50, 48, 52.

23 General Valuation Office, *Revised valuation books*.

24 *Census of Ireland 1901, pt. i: giving details of the area, houses and population; vol. i, province of Leinster* p. 17 [Cd. 847–VIII], H.C. 1902, cxiii, 123.

25 See for example, *Drogheda Independent*, 11 Feb. 1905, 1 April 1905.

26 *General valuation . . . union of Dunshaughlin.*

27 *Report from the select committee appointed to inquire into the state of Westmeath and the nature of a certain unlawful combination existing therein, with proceedings, minutes of evidence, appendix and index,* p. 111, H.C. 1871 (147), xiii, 667. (Cited hereafter as *Select committee into the state of Westmeath*).

28 NA, Census of Ireland 1901, Enumerators' forms, Co. Meath, DEDs 10, 14 and 19.

29 See Enda McKay, 'The housing of the rural labourer, 1883–1916' in *Saothar,* xvii (1992), pp 27–38.

30 *Royal commission on labour, reports by assistant commissioners on the agricultural labourer, pt. ii, reports by Mr. W.P. O'Brien,* p. 31 [C 6894–xix], H.C. 1893–94, xxxvii, pt. 1, 101.

31 *Census of Ireland, 1911, pt. ii: general report, with tables and appendix,* p. x [Cd. 6663], H.C. 1912–13, cxviii, 10.

32 David Fitzpatrick, 'The disappearance of the Irish agricultural labourer, 1841–1912' in *Irish Economic and Social History,* vii (1980), pp 80.

33 *Report of the poor law inspectors on the wages of agricultural labourers in Ireland,* p. 17 [C 35], H.C. 1870, xiv, 19.

34 *Select committee into the state of Westmeath,* p. 111.

35 *Royal commission on labour, pt. iv,* p. 364.

36 *Agricultural statistics . . . 1901,* p. 148.

37 *Agricultural statistics of Ireland, with detailed reports for the year 1902,* pp 151–2 [Cd 1614], H.C. 1903, lxxxii, 517–8.

38 *Agricultural statistics of Ireland . . . 1901,* p. 325.

39 *Royal commission on labour, pt. iv,* p. 139.

40 *Agricultural statistics of Ireland, with a detailed report on agriculture, for the year 1896,* pp 98–9 [C 8510], H.C. 1897, xcviii, 456–7.

41 Calculations based on *Abstract of answers and returns under the population acts, enumeration 1831,* pp 72–3, 80–1, H.C. 1833 (634), xxxix, 131–2, 139–40 and NA, Census of Ireland 1901, Enumerators' forms, Co. Meath, DEDs 10, 14, 19.

42 *Royal commission on labour,* pt. iv, p. 25.

43 General Valuation Office, *Revised valuation books.*

A DECADE OF CONFLICT, 1904–14

1 See Table 1.

2 Calculated from *Agricultural statistics of Ireland, 1901,* pp 25, 39.

3 Jones, *Graziers, land reform and political conflict,* p. 241.

4 *Meath Herald,* 14 September 1907.

5 *Drogheda Independent,* 5 January 1907.

6 Bulfin, *Rambles in Eirinn,* p. 89.

7 Figures in this and the following paragraph are calculated from NA, Census of Ireland 1901, Enumerators' forms, Co. Meath, DEDs 10, 14 and 19.

8 Jones, *Graziers, land reform and political conflict,* p. 246.

9 Geary, *The plan of campaign,* p. 79.

10 Jones, *Graziers, land reform and political conflict,* pp 126–7.

11 *Select committee into the state of Westmeath,* p. 86.

12 NA, LEC Rentals, vol. 149, no. 61, 6 November 1885.

13 *Drogheda Independent,* 17 March 1906.

14 *Meath Herald,* 16 February 1907.

15 Laurence Ginnell, *Land and liberty,* (Dublin, 1908), p. 213.

16 *Meath Herald,* 9 November 1907.

17 *Meath Herald,* 26 October 1907.

18 *Meath Herald* and *Drogheda Independent,* 9 November 1907.

19 NA, Crime Branch Special, Intelligence notes, box no. 2, 1907, 127, quoted in Paul Bew, *Conflict and conciliation in Ireland, 1890–1910,* (Oxford, 1987), p. 135.

20 NLI, Colonial Office Papers, Police reports, Jan.–April 1909, CO 904/77/822.

21 *Return of untenanted lands in rural districts, distinguishing demesnes on which there is a mansion, showing (1) rural district and electoral division; (2) townland; (3) area in statute acres; (4) valuation (poor law); (5) names of occupiers, as in valuation lists,* H.C. 1906, (250), c, 177. (Cited hereafter as *Return of untenanted lands*).

22 *Final report of the royal commission appointed to inquire into and report upon the operation of the acts dealing with congestion in Ireland,* p. 45 [Cd 4097], H.C. 1908, xlii, 785.

23 *Drogheda Independent,* 6 November 1909, 15 January 1910.

24 *Drogheda Independent,* 14 May 1910 and 15 April 1914.

25 *Return of untenanted lands,* pp 160–2.

26 RD, 1862 /10/135

27 See third chapter above.

28 *Drogheda Independent,* 10 January 1914.

29 General Valuation Office, Revised valuation books, no. 1, Killeen ED.

30 *Return of the names of proprietors and the area and valuation of all properties in the several counties in Ireland, held in fee or perpetuity or on long leases at chief rents,* p. 29, H.C. 1876 (412), lxxx, 423.

31 *Meath Chronicle,* 20 and 27 February 1904.

32 See note 56, chapter 3.

33 *Burke's peerage and baronetage,* (105th ed., 2nd impression, London, 1975), p. 1912 and *General valuation . . . Union of Dunshaughlin,* p. 12.

34 *Drogheda Independent,* 14 April 1914.

35 General Valuation Office, Revised valuation books.

36 Oliver Coogan, *Politics and war in Meath, 1913–23,* (Dublin, 1983), p. 23.

37 NLI, MS 708, Minute book of the national directory of the United Irish League, 10 Aug. 1904–30 April 1918. Affiliation fee of £3 was paid in 1905, 1908 and 1914 only. (Cited hereafter as Minute book of the United Irish League).

38 *Meath Herald,* 31 August 1907.

39 *Meath Chronicle,* 22 February 1908.

40 Bew, *Conflict and conciliation,* pp 156–8, 163–6.

41 *Meath Chronicle,* 17 August 1907.

42 *Drogheda Independent,* 31 August 1907 and *Meath Chronicle,* 31 August 1907.

43 *Meath Chronicle,* 6 June 1908 and *Drogheda Independent,* 18 July 1908.

44 *Drogheda Independent,* 17 March 1906.

45 *Return in respect to labourers' cottages in Ireland, showing the number of cottages applied for in each Poor Law Union in Ireland under the latest completed scheme in connection with the Labourers' (Ireland) Acts . . . to the 31st day of March 1906,* pp 4–5, H.C. 1906 (193), civ, 650–1. (Cited hereafter as *Return in respect to labourers' cottages*).

46 *Annual report of the Local Government Board for Ireland for the year ended 31st March 1908,* pp xliii, 269–71 [Cd 4243], H.C. 1907–08, xxxi, 61, 339–41.

47 *Drogheda Independent,* 24 February 1906, 29 December 1906.

48 *Drogheda Independent,* 12 January 1907.

49 *Drogheda Independent,* 30 March 1907.

50 *Drogheda Independent,* 19 September 1908.

51 *Return in respect to labourers' cottages,* pp 4–5.

52 Minute book of the United Irish League, 8 February 1909, p. 293, 7 February 1912, p. 415.

53 *Census of Ire., 1911, ii,* p. xxi.

54 Calculations based on NA, Census 1911, Enumerators' forms, Co. Meath, DEDs 10, 14 and 19.

55 *Agricultural statistics, Ireland 1911. Report and tables relating to Irish agricultural labourers,* pp 10, 34 [Cd 6198], H.C. 1912–13, cvi, 1062, 1086.

56 *Drogheda Independent,* 8 September 1906.

57 *Drogheda Independent*, 31 January
    1914.
58 Coogan, *Politics and war in Meath*, p.
    246.
59 *Meath Herald*, 7 May 1907, 30
    November 1907.
60 Murray's public house and general
    store, Sales ledger 1900–02,

manuscript records in the custody
of Mr. Brendan Murray, Grangend,
Dunshaughlin, pp 101, 175, 12.

CONCLUSION

1 *Drogheda Independent*, August 31 1907.